Literacy Online

New Tools for Struggling Readers and Writers

DISCARDED

Julie M. Wood

Foreword by
VICTORIA PURCELL-GATES

HEINEMANN
Portsmouth, NH

Heinemann
A division of Reed Elsevier Inc.
361 Hanover Street
Portsmouth, NH 03801–3912
www.heinemann.com

Offices and agents throughout the world

Library of Congress Cataloging-in-Publication Data
Wood, Julie M.
    Literacy online : new tools for struggling readers and writers / Julie M. Wood.
       p. cm.
    Includes bibliographical references.
    ISBN 0-325-00369-6 (alk. paper)
    1. Language arts (Elementary)—Computer-assisted instruction.
2. Internet in education.   3. Computers and literacy.   4. Language
arts—Remedial teaching.   I. Title.

LB1576.7.W66 2004
372.6'078'5—dc22   2004007842

Editor: Lisa Barnett
Production service: Lisa S. Garboski, bookworks
Production coordinator: Lynne Reed
Cover design: Night & Day Design
Cover illustration: John A. Wood
Typesetter: TechBooks
Manufacturing: Steve Bernier

Printed in the United States of America on acid-free paper
08 07 06 05 04 MV 1 2 3 4 5

CONTENTS

CONTENTS

FOREWORD

This is a timely and important book for teachers and for teacher educators. In an era of multiliteracies, on-line reading and writing is finally taking its rightful place on center stage, along with paper-based literacies and media literacies. Locating on-line literacies within the discourse of reading and writing development, as Julie Wood has done, makes this text of special importance to teachers. Yes, reading and writing development do occur in the process of reading and writing on-line, just as well, if not more effectively, as with paper-based texts. This book offers research and theory to support this claim. More importantly, though, it offers teachers many rich examples of on-line learning along with a multitude of suggestions and resources.

The content of this book must be understood within the context of the literacy instructional theory and practice within which many of the principles and experiences, related in the book, were developed. Without this context, one could conclude that Chall's Stages of Reading Development lead naturally to the authentic online reading and writing activities Wood advocates for. With this context provided, readers can fill in the historical and pedagogical gaps that link Chall's important foundational work and Wood's online literacy theory and practice.

READING BECOMES LITERACY

Wood describes a year in the life of the Harvard Literacy Lab, during which she conducted her research on which this book is based. The name—*Literacy* Lab—was assumed in 1992 as a change from the original—*Reading* Lab. This name change was not a trivial matter and, in many ways, signifies the theoretical and pedagogical changes that had, and were, occurring in the field of literacy instruction. I had assumed the directorship of the Harvard Reading Lab in 1991, upon the retirement of Dr. Chall, its founder. Part of my charge was to transform the Reading Lab in ways that reflected current research and theory in the field. While numerous curricular changes were conceived and implemented by me and other literacy faculty at the Harvard Graduate School of Education, the course that connected graduate students to the Lab as teachers and the pedagogy instantiated in the Lab underwent significant changes.

As the term *literacy* reflects, *writing* development became as much of a focus for assessment and instruction as *reading* development. This move reflected current theory and practice that saw the development of writing skills and attitude as crucial and previously unattended to by schools and teachers, relative to the attention given to reading. Much research was occurring on the development of writing ability at the time, and many publications were available for teachers, often written by teachers. In addition, current research was providing deeper insights into the reading/writing connections than ever before. As teachers, we could see more clearly how learning to write helped one learn to read and vice versa. By renaming the Reading Lab as the Literacy Lab, we could publicly assume this writing/reading stance as well as more accurately label the diagnostic and instructional activities that were conducted therein.

Beyond this shift to include writing into the pedagogy of the Lab, though, the assumption of the term *literacy* also reflected a deep theoretical shift in the field. *Literacy*, as a label for a field of research and practice, encompasses a broader field than does *Reading*, or even *Reading/Writing*. The term *literacy* denotes a language practice that is cultural, social, cognitive, historically constructed, and ultimately defined by relationships of power. Thus, the "field of literacy" is informed by research and knowledge from such disciplines as psychology, linguistics, sociology, history, anthropology, and education. Course content for the graduate students who taught in the Harvard Literacy Lab reflected this breadth of knowledge. Upon vote of the faculty, the *Harvard Reading Lab* became the *Harvard Literacy Lab*.

As you read in the coming chapters the many descriptions of the opportunities computers offer for engaging writing activities, my hope is that this brief history of the evolution of the Literacy Lab's name will enlighten and provide historical and theoretical context for these activities. Another pedagogical change, though, also contextualized Wood's Lab experience and research, and its import requires explanation.

AUTHENTIC READING AND WRITING

With this broader view of literacy came the notion of *authentic reading and writing*. The definition of authentic reading/writing was loose and fuzzy but the term was being used a lot during the 1990s and during my tenure as director of the Literacy Lab. At its core, the term meant reading or writing of "real" texts as contrasted with doing isolated skill work or skill work that involved "artificial" texts, constructed for the purpose of learning skills. The instructional approach I brought into the Literacy Lab was one I termed

Whole-Part-Whole. This looks very close to what is now referred to as Balanced Literacy Instruction. The essence of this approach is to teach skills in the context of authentic reading and writing.

With this instructional approach, I built on Chall's view that once children learned to decode, they need to read books a great deal to develop fluency and automaticity. I expanded and clarified this (again, reflecting much of the current research and practice at the time) to make authentic reading and writing a central part of all literacy instruction, including that directed toward beginning readers and writers. I also brought my definition of authentic reading and writing into the Lab.

At the time, this definition was not fully clarified to the degree that I could put it into definitional language, but I could describe it enough to ensure that my students learned to incorporate authentic literacy into their instruction of children. Since that time, I have conducted several large-scale research studies that have shown statistically significant outcomes of authentic literacy instruction for both adults and children.[1] In the process, a definition has emerged that allows one to assess a particular literacy instructional activity and judge the degree to which it is authentic.

We conceptualize authentic literacy events as those that replicate or reflect reading and writing events that occur in the world outside of a schooling context. An authentic literacy event is, thus, a communicative event and as such involves two interlocutors—each event has a writer and a reader or a reader of a writer. To judge the authenticity of a literacy event, we look at two dimensions of the event—*purpose/function* and *text*. Authentic *purpose or function* means that the literacy event serves a communicative purpose, like reading to answer questions or writing to provide information for someone who wants or needs it, in addition to learning particular skills or content. To be authentic, a *text* (written or read) must be like, or very much like, texts that are used by readers and writers outside of a learning to read or write context to serve communicative purposes or functions.

Authentic literacy events/activities, thus, involve students in reading or writing textual forms that occur in the lives of literate people for the purposes that literate people read and write them, *in addition to, or aside from,*

---

[1] Purcell-Gates, V., Degener, S., Jacobson, E., & Soler, M. (2002). Impact of authentic literacy instruction on adult literacy practices. *Reading Research Quarterly, 37,* 70–92. Also, Purcell-Gates, V., Duke, N.K., Hall, L., & Tower, C. (2003). *Explicit Explanation of Genre Within Authentic Literacy Activities in Science: Does it Facilitate Development and Achievement?* Paper presented at the 2003 National Reading Conference, Scottsdale, AZ.

learning to read and/or write. Those texts and reading/writing purposes that reflect primarily literacy learning purposes are counter posed to authentic texts and purposes, and we refer to these as *school-only* texts and purposes. Examples of *authentic texts/purposes* include reading a newspaper for information, writing a personal letter to a friend to maintain friendship and share personal information, reading a novel for relaxation and/or to discuss with a book group, writing an information book about Dolphins to include in the class library for others to read for information, or reading a health pamphlet to learn ways to protect one's health.

Examples of school-only textual forms and purposes include writing a list of words for a spelling test, reading a passage and answering comprehension questions, writing a report on worms to turn in to the teacher for a grade, reading a decodable text to practice just-learned phonics rules, and writing to fill in the blanks on a skill worksheet. At times, one finds authentic texts read for school-only purposes such as when students may be asked to read a newspaper story and find all of the long vowel words or to circle the compound sentences. As stated earlier, research is beginning to document the positive effect on development of involving children in authentic reading and writing in the process of literacy instruction.

AUTHENTIC LITERACY IN THE LITERACY LAB

You will find many examples throughout this book of ways to use technology to facilitate authentic reading and writing while at the same time helping children get a hold of the essential skills needed to learn to read and write. These include such activities as using digital photos to create photo journals to be read by others as part of phonics lessons, capturing Readers' Theatre readings on a camcorder for later showings to an audience, composing and sending emails around the world to new friends, online publishing of texts for others to read and enjoy or learn from, and many, many more. As first a Teaching Fellow and then a Director in the Harvard Literacy Lab, Julie Wood developed her ideas about the possibilities of the marriage of literacy learning and technology within an historically situated theoretical and pedagogical context. The conceptualization of literacy as more than reading and a growing awareness of the role of authentic reading/writing in successful literacy development were, in my opinion, critical to this context.

Victoria Purcell–Gates
Canada Research Chair of Early Childhood Literacy
University of British Columbia

ACKNOWLEDGMENTS

I awoke this morning with devout thanksgiving for my friends,
the old and the new.
—Ralph Waldo Emerson

Today is Thanksgiving. It seems to me to be the perfect day to acknowledge all the people in my life who have helped me along the way as I've written this book. To each one of them, I am deeply thankful.

First there are the teachers, students, and parents who participated in the Literacy Lab the year I served as director. Each of you taught me more than I can say. And I can still picture each of you in my mind's eye—exactly the way you were that year. Special thanks to Nicole Jernée and Kristin Kellogg for documenting the work of two students, "Richard" and "Jackie," respectively. They wrote with enthusiasm and were always there for me, ready to exchange ideas and help me get it right. I'm also in deep debt to our two outstanding Teaching Fellows, Julie Park and Natalie LaCroix White.

Then there are the talented wordsmiths who helped me conceptualize what I wanted to say and helped me say it better. My superb editor at Heinemann, Danny Miller, who was always there "in the ether," even though he lives 3,000 miles away, and who has the patience of a saint; my colleague Ray Coutu, who critiqued my first book proposal over lunch in Harvard Square; stellar copy editor Carol Kort, who read early, *really* rough drafts without flinching—as did David Gordon of Harvard Education Press, each over several cups of coffee, which was important since much energy was required at that stage.

Many friends and colleagues over the years offered encouragement and sustenance. Without their support I simply would have keeled over. They include Marilyn Jager Adams, Linda Caswell, Chris Dede, Cheryl Dressler, Nell Duke, Ilona Holland, Carla Innerfield, Vicki Jacobs, Connie Juel, Glen Kleiman, Linda Krain, Sheila Kramer, Andrea Oseas, Carol Philips, Victoria Purcell-Gates, Catherine Snow, Evangeline Stefanakis, Patti Sullivan-Hall, Patton Tabors, Stone Wiske, and Judy Zorfass.

ACKNOWLEDGMENTS

Members of my women's book group, the Bitchin' Book Babes, had more influence over my work than they know; I was terrified of having my book receive the sort of salty reviews that we as a group casually dished out each month when critiquing the books we had read.

Affectionate thanks to my family for enduring my writerly angst and encouraging me when I needed it most. I am indebted to you, Georgia Wood, Crispin Wood, Will Riddell, Justine Covault, and Rick, Maureen, Jessica, and Brielle Laffey. And at the very summit of the list is my husband, John A. Wood—muse, best friend, and, as it happens, the illustrator of this book.

Julie M. Wood
Cambridge, Massachusetts

A Thought on Gratitude

Let us be grateful to people who make us happy: They are the charming gardeners who make our souls blossom.
—Marcel Proust

Literacy Writ Large Using New Tools

I FEEL LIKE I'VE SEEN THE CURTAIN GO UP ON THE TWENTY-first century. Educators all over the country, perhaps including you, have been challenged by the need to develop students' literacy skills not just for today's world, but for the world they'll encounter in 2020. But how should you go about it? This is the $64,000 question that motivated me to attend the Technology Showcase at the Watertown Middle School, in Watertown, Massachusetts, recently. "Come see what WE know about computers!" the electronic invitation read. I could hardly resist.

For the past five years Watertown Public Schools have been involved in a program called MetroLINC, a technology initiative sponsored mainly by a Technology Innovations Challenge Grant (U.S. Department of Education). The mission of the grant was to explore the question of how to integrate new computers and other gadgets into existing curricula. The Technology Showcase was a chance to show off the results—thirty-five exhibits created by students from every grade level (K–12).

I was dazzled by the exhibits students presented that day. Electronic jewelry. That is, earrings and necklaces in the shape of flowers that students programmed to flash bright colors.[1] Little "towers" that students carried around to power their electronic inventions. A mask with electronic eyeballs that changed color. An iMovie of an original production of *A Midsummer Night's Dream*. A video journal featuring interviews with graduating seniors, created by students from the resource room.

Electronic gear (see in particular the hat and necklace) created by students with the help of technology experts at MIT.

The Showcase was held in the Middle School Library. Students of every description "worked" their booths, eager to talk to passersby about their projects. Literacy learning was evident everywhere. Jennifer Balabanian, the first girl I chatted with, became animated when she described her project centered on her teachers' favorite poetry. When I asked why she chose this subject, Jennifer replied, "I decided to do this because I thought kids had stereotypes about teachers liking long, boring poems. So I surveyed all the teachers and I came up with the conclusion that teachers like poems that suit their personalities. Like Mr. Smith is crazy and wacky, so his favorite poem is 'Jabberwocky,' by Lewis Carroll. Miss Martinez is all about respect. You can tell she wants to go somewhere in life so her favorite poem is by Ralph Waldo Emerson." Technology came into play when Jennifer searched online for the text of teachers' favorite poems, and again when she created a PowerPoint ™ presentation to organize and display her work.

As I glanced around the Library, evidence of students' development as readers and writers was hard to miss. For instance, one group of boys learned that in Shakespeare's time men played female roles because women were banned from the stage. With Monty Python–like aplomb, the male actors had dressed in gowns for a performance of *A Midsummer Night's Dream*. They vamped around in low-cut satin dresses with their pant legs and sneakers on full display just below their hemlines. But more important, the boys learned how to interpret the roles they played. Each one tried to plumb the depths of his character. Since in this class's production girls also played key roles, students compared notes with peers in Minnesota who were producing the same play. They also exchanged videotapes of their performances. That meant that a boy playing the part of Puck or Demetrius, let's say, could discuss his interpretation with a boy from the Midwest who was playing the same role. According to their teacher, Ms. McDonagh, this project also served as a catalyst for learning about stage production, video editing, and the specialized vocabulary words that go with each. They also learned to use digital cameras to capture their tableaus of dramatic scenes.

It was clear that the students were not the only learners in this *Midsummer Night's Dream* production; Ms. McDonagh made a few intellectual leaps of her own. For example, she traveled to Washington, D.C., for a National Endowment for the Humanities institute called "Teaching Shakespeare" at the Folger Shakespeare Library.[2] She became so inspired that she wrote an article about her experience that appeared in *Shakespeare Magazine.*

Another cluster of middle school students I chatted with came to understand their grandparents' history as part of a social studies project. Through interviews, students documented their grandparents' first-person accounts of what it was like to live through World War II and/or Vietnam. To tap into their grandparents' recollections, students learned to conduct interviews. As part of their training they critiqued videotapes of their teachers purposely making all the classic interview mistakes, such as not asking follow-up questions. As Ms. McDonagh, also the teacher for this project, remarked, "Oral history is a project we've had for many years—students interview someone over sixty, generally a family member. We're studying history and English together, so this is the marriage of those two subjects. So they're looking at all the elements that make culture, culture. Everything from political events in one's life to one's values. We look at cultural generalizations. We look at how those issues have changed over two generations." To be able to do this, their teacher continued, "[s]tudents need to learn interviewing skills, they have to plan the interview, they have to take notes. They have to transcribe. . . . We also did an iMovie. We played with this. We tried to do a tape with digital sound." All these skills the teacher describes speak volumes about what new literacies look like in action.

"They [students] got a lot out of it," Ms. McDonagh continued. "It was a really rich experience. First and foremost it was about getting to know their grandparents better. They have a better sense of the world based on what we're learning. We learned about war, and we interviewed someone who lived through one. We learned how to use interview skills... They did research on the time period... The best thing they took away from this is learning how to put so many different ideas and skills together for the final project." Clearly students have learned how to use new media to read, interpret what they learn, conduct research, and communicate their ideas.

Then there was Mr. Gustafson's Renaissance Project for high school students. When I asked one young woman, Lisa, about her project she replied, "I learned all about Michelangelo's life and about his paintings. And I learned how to use PowerPoint." When I asked about this software, she remarked, "I never used it before. I've always had it on my

computer but I never used it. It turned out to be really good. I use it a lot now."

When I asked Lisa how this project affected her learning, she said, "I have a digital camera that I bring with me everywhere I go. I can take pictures of my friends and stuff and create a whole slide show."

Behind Lisa is a handmade poster proclaiming, "These are the tools we worked with." Beneath the heading, in handwriting, was this list: "HyperStudio, PowerPoint, videos, web based research, audiotaping, CD production, music, Internet, animation, and word processor."

Mr. Gustafson joined us. He reflected on his own learning curve stating "It [technology] allows me to bring in some materials I wouldn't be able to do otherwise. So we go to virtual museums . . . instead of asking kids to try to *imagine* what some of these artifacts look like."

Mr. Gustafson described a project one student designed for his study of Leonardo DaVinci. The young man created his own film, in which he interviewed a friend who played the role of DaVinci. Of the student's work, Mr. Gustafson remarked, "He wrote a script, he did the research, he found the location, and then he had a very high level, mostly scripted, conversation. So it [the availability of technology] brings a lot more of personalization to a project that they would have otherwise." Again, new literacies are evolving in middle school classrooms.

Mr. Gustafson's own experience with computers harks back to the early days of zeroes and ones. When I asked him what it is like to use technology for class projects, he replied, "It's a lot of extra work. I have to learn a little about everything I'm using technology-wise to be able to help kids achieve their dream." His current project is learning how to use Dreamweaver software to create websites.

In describing his early experiences with computers, Mr. Gustafson recalled, "When I went to high school in the late 1970s, early '80s, the idea of using computers in the classroom was really new. Now it's almost expected. The first computer I worked on was a computer built by Wang. We used the four-digit coding. I remember 0206. That was the command for print. And whatever the next thing you coded, it would print that character. So if you wanted to print the letter A, that was 0001. So you had to type 0206, then 0001. Two lines of code; eight characters. It would print the letter A. Then if you wanted to do another letter next to it, to spell a word, then it was another print, another letter, another print, return." Smiling ruefully he recalled, "It took hundreds of lines of code to print simple instructions that would produce a graphic. It was tedious. Now I take a movie, drag, boom! convert it for export, burn it on CD, burn it back to a videotape—it's all very easy." So easy, in fact, that probably every student in the room could convert movies to CD-ROMs and back again without breaking a sweat.

I met two seniors who had studied Cuban culture in their Spanish class. Mary remarked, "We watched a movie about the hardships they have there. My teacher got in touch with people from Cuba. We did research. It was an eye-opener for me because of all the stuff that we take for granted that some people don't have." To deepen their cultural understanding, students began email exchanges with peers in Cuba. In this way they were developing their writing skills in a genuine context.

Although an hour had passed, I had only scratched the surface. I never did get to visit the "Café au Paris" project, which included multimedia reports. I never did see the "Using Technology Tools" or "The Life-cycle of the Butterfly." Time had run out, speeches were given, and raffle numbers were drawn for fancy headsets and other digital gadgetry.

Strictly speaking, none of what I saw that afternoon was cutting edge. There were of course the electronic jewelry and mask a small subset of students had created with help from professors at the Massachusetts Institute of Technology, but PowerPoint, iMovies, digital images, and the Internet ruled the day—tools that have become commonplace in many reading and language arts classrooms. Nobody claimed that students' projects were the stuff of futuristic fantasies. Instead, the projects had a sincere, down to earth quality about them. Students and teachers alike have been finding their own compass for how to do this sort of thing. The projects were like the first pancake, so to speak—overcooked or underdone, practice for the fluffy, perfectly browned pancakes that will be served up in the next batch.

As much as I reveled in visiting the booths, in truth I only skimmed the surface. And yet what I saw that day, in just sixty minutes, was transcendent. As a society we are in the throes of transition, particularly in conceptualizing what it means to be literate in today's world. The sorts of reading, writing, and other forms of communication I witnessed at the Technology Showcase offered insights into where teachers and students are *now*, not just in Watertown, but across the country. And where they are now matters because each individual is on the cusp of being someplace else very soon. When I squinted just a little bit, just enough to blur the colors and voices into one large, kinetic abstraction, I began to see the rough outlines of the future of literacy learning. Squinting a little harder, taking in all the digital projects and their proud developers, I swear I caught a glimpse of the world students will inhabit in 2020.

These students and their peers all over the country are part of a generation that believes that technology can help them do more than learn facts. Technology can do more than add pixel dust to the usual projects about Shakespeare or butterflies. Each project announced a new take on using reading and writing to develop important ideas. Anyone could see that this generation understands that technology can help them better understand the vastness of the universe, who they are, and how their unique personalities fit into the grand scheme.

That's why it's worth doing. That's why we as teachers need to be on the vanguard of change today, in the digital age.

ENDNOTES

1. Several students worked on "digital manipulatives" with professors from the MIT Media Lab as part of a "Lifelong Kindergarten" project. According to the MIT website, the goal is this: "Our new digital versions of these toys [such as the jewelry and the mask] enable children to explore a new set of concepts (in particular, 'systems concepts' such as feedback and emergence) that have previously been considered 'too advanced' for children to learn." For more information see *llk.media.mit. edu/projects/summaries/toys.shtml*.

2. The Folger Shakespeare Museum: *www.folger.edu/Home_02B.html*.

1
PART
Literacy in the Digital Age

In the Industrial Age, schools were isolated from the rest of their communities, when the knowledge to be mastered could be contained in textbooks and teachers' lectures at the blackboard. In the Digital Age, most knowledge lies beyond the classroom walls, requiring that the artificial barriers between school and community be dismantled.
—Milton Chen[1]

More than ever before, teachers are being called upon not only to teach but also to help change the world. The technological revolution has swept into our lives bringing about changes that I'll bet even Marshall McLuhan, once referred to as the Oracle of the Electronic Age, wouldn't have predicted thirty or forty years ago. Along with the technological revolution come new tools that are vital to the way we teach and the way we live. These new tools are reshaping our society in ways so profound that we have yet to realize their full potential.

In Part 1 of this book I invite you to reflect on what it means for a student to be literate in the twenty-first century. How should we rethink our teaching accordingly? What resources can we draw upon? What conceptual frameworks can time-honored theorists, such as Lev Vygotsky and John Dewey, offer to help us find our way? How can we rise to some of today's educational challenges with the same enlightened determination as the Founding Fathers, who also took the long view? They, after all, considered the consequences of their actions far beyond the here and now.

In Part 2, I focus on seven essential literacy skills, why many students struggle in attaining them, recommended practices, and how new technologies can be used to enhance your teaching in each skill area. The seven essential skills I've zeroed in on are those that have the greatest impact on students' literacy development: word recognition, fluency, comprehension, vocabulary, reading and writing across the curriculum, process writing, and motivation.

In Part 3, I present you with a case study of one year in a university-based Reading Laboratory. I describe what happened when my graduate students and I gave struggling readers and writers the opportunity to publish their original compositions on their own web page and correspond with people all over the world. I'll show you actual examples of how students actually appropriated new tools for their own purposes, depending on their social, emotional, and pedagogical needs. The great news is that they became more proficient readers and writers in the process. I hope that our experiences will inspire you to use telecommunication tools to connect your students with the larger world—to, in Chen's words, dismantle the barriers between school and community.

In Part 4, I turn the spotlight on you, challenging *you* to become innovators in *your* district as part and parcel of literacy professional in the digital age. I offer analytical tools to help you analyze where you've been, where you are now, where you want to be, and the steps you'll need to take to realize your vision.

THE MAGIC OF KIDS AND COMPUTERS

Kids love gadgets. They love to get their hands on gears and wheels and push and pull and see what happens. I reflected on this simple truth when my fourth-graders, in the precomputer era, elbowed each other out of the way to get to the old typewriter I installed in a learning center. My students were also enthralled by listening to their recorded voices on a tape recorder as well as listening to recordings of the books.

I had read aloud, on tape. The simplest machines had the power to entrance them (think of Pez dispensers!).

A teacher in the 1970s could get by with very little in the way of gadgets. The occasional filmstrip on Lewis and Clark, the reel-to-reel film about how paper was made seemed to do the trick. Sometimes we'd even dim the lights and hover around a large black-and-white television set watching a program on children's literature ("Looks at Books") before anyone ever conceived of the more sophisticated "Reading Rainbow" and its splendid treatment of books.

Today, of course, we have a much more powerful tool—the computer. Things *happen* when you use a computer; time is measured in nanoseconds rather than minutes. To click a mouse is to get an immediate response.

From a child's point of view the computer is as magical as an invisibility cloak, flying broomstick, or any wizardry dreamed up by J. K. Rowling, the popular author of the Harry Potter series. No wonder children are enchanted by them; computers are fun. Using them makes you feel incredibly cool.

When it comes to writing on a computer, kids far prefer it to writing on paper. Not surprising! Writing on paper is hard; not only is it hard for young children to form letters orthographically, they're also expected to write neatly within margins. And when they make mistakes they need to erase them cleanly, and there's the rub. Erasures often result in torn paper and the child is left with an embarrassingly illegible mess. Kids are smart. They know that these untidy papers can't convey their ideas in a way they can be proud of. In contrast, when they compose on the screen, their work looks dignified. They can use spell-check and grammar software to edit their writing. Their compositions, whether a quick email message or a full-blown report on Brazil, look professional. Above all, through word processors, children immediately gain entry into the adult world of print.

This is not to say that we want kids to be seduced by computers; that we want them to be automatons who are allergic to writing with pencils or paper. But as educators we really do need to take a closer look at the computer's ability to transfix young learners and get them excited about learning. If we could make reading and writing as much fun as playing Nintendo, we'd be halfway there!

What does the advent of the digital age look like when we take the long view, that is, the *really* long view over several millennia?

"PUNCTUATED EQUILIBRIUM"

In reflecting on how the new educational media have evolved over time, evolutionary biologist Stephen Jay Gould comes to mind. It was Gould who shook up the scientific community with his theory of punctuated equilibrium as it affects biological evolution. Gould challenged the existing theory of continuous evolutionary change, arguing that the fossil record in fact reveals long periods of equilibrium punctuated by *quick bursts of evolution* when the environment changed significantly.[2]

Gould's theory of punctuated equilibrium offers us another way to think about the effects of new educational technologies on students and teaching. Over the past eighty years technological innovation has not significantly changed how we teach in schools. A backward glance shows that chalkboards and chalk have stubbornly remained the most popular teaching tools for hundreds of years.[3] Yes, there have been more innovations than we can count, but *fundamental* changes that have really penetrated core educational practices are rare.[4]

In contrast, the recent impact of digital technologies has been seismic—throwing schools into a quick burst of evolution.[5] The old ways of doing things have been challenged. It's no wonder that veteran teachers sometimes feel like so many dinosaurs on the verge of becoming extinct.

A reading/language arts teacher could be forgiven for being skeptical about the lasting effects of this quick burst of evolution. They could question whether digital technologies have really improved literacy instruction, or if they just added glitz to the surface. Many have argued, in fact, that if all the computers and other electronic gadgets were removed tomorrow, schools would recover rapidly. The loss would not be devastating because new tools, for the most part, haven't yet entered the bloodstream of classroom life. They've remained on the outer fringes of teaching and learning like so many unloved, flashy gadgets destined for yard sales. (Remember the videodisc?)

But the digital age has thrown teachers and schools into a quick burst of evolution. If you listen hard enough you can hear the subtle shifts in gears that make schools run. When it comes to new literacies— visual literacy, information literacy, media literacy—many teachers are eager to learn how best to take advantage of new tools to improve instruction. These teachers are at the forefront of change.

LEVELING THE PLAYING FIELD FOR YOUR STUDENTS

My hunch is that teachers who are willing to reinvent themselves also believe in the promise of a more democratic society. Although it may sound idealistic, teachers who use new tools well *can* level the playing field. Think of Horace Mann's astute observation: "Education, then, beyond all other devices of human origin, is the great equalizer of the conditions of man—the balance-wheel of the social machinery." Is it reasonable to think that technology can become the great equalizer teachers have sought over the last century? From my own research and that of my colleagues, I think the answer is a resounding YES. Access to digital technologies can offer children in poverty many of the same benefits as their peers in wealthier districts. They can definitely help underserved children learn to read and write. In so doing, new tools can help erase the boundaries between the haves and have nots. Technology *can*, in Mann's words, equalize the conditions of humankind provided that *all* students have unfettered access to new tools and training. Without access and training, new tools pose a barrier to academic achievement and future prosperity for children in underserved communities.

Recent statistics about the availability of new tools are encouraging, even in low socioeconomic settings. The poorest sector of society is now the fastest-growing group to gain access to computers and the Internet. Also encouraging is the fact that public schools have more access to new tools than ever before. Access alone, of course, doesn't necessarily lead to quality learning; many other factors, such as sophisticated reading and writing skills, come into play. But when you consider that currently 57 percent of all jobs and 80 percent of managerial positions require computer skills, it's heartening to know that many more students have a shot at bridging the digital divide today than they did just a decade ago.[6]

SPECIAL NEEDS CALL FOR SPECIAL TOOLS

In addition to redressing the digital divide, new tools can help your at-risk students with individual needs become proficient readers and writers. For example, children who are visually impaired can use special filters when using the Internet. Among other virtues, the filters allow students to adjust the size and color of the font and have text read to them aloud. Children with learning disabilities can use word processing capabilities to help them rearrange their ideas as they compose their ideas and then flesh them out with supporting details by simply cutting and pasting chunks of text. They can also highlight text, check their spelling, and access an online dictionary and thesaurus with just a few keystrokes. Children who have motor difficulties can use a specially adapted mouse and keyboard, and other adaptive hardware. New solutions are being developed for students with individual needs every day (see, for example, LD Online at *ldonline.org*).[7]

Consider also your chronically disorganized students—the ones whose messy desks and backpacks make it nearly impossible for them to retrieve homework assignments. Such students often have terrific ideas but encounter great difficulties when asked to write them down. Often their compositions lack an organizational scheme—a framework that they can use to develop complex ideas. You can show students how to use software products, such as Inspiration, to help them create graphic organizers electronically. These organizers, with their graphic representations (e.g., webs and flowcharts), can help students visualize information. For example, students can create a visual hierarchy that they can draw on in distinguishing between main ideas and supporting details. (See technology specialist Sandy Beck's website for specific ideas about creating graphic organizers on your computer.)[8]

MULTIPLE INTELLIGENCES THEORY CAN GUIDE YOUR USE OF NEW TECHNOLOGIES

Another rationale for using new tools is that they can offer you a powerful way to cultivate students' cognitive abilities as you teach them to read and write. That is, you can figure out what children are good at—mathematical reasoning, art, writing fiction—and then capitalize on their strengths. If you're familiar with Howard Gardner's theory of multiple intelligences (MI), then you understand that the brain has eight different domains, or intelligences, rather than one monolithic IQ that's based solely on linguistic and computational skills, as shown in the accompanying box.

Multiple Intelligences, as Defined by Howard Gardner[9]

The eight intelligences, or ways we can learn, can work synergistically.

- Logical/mathematical (mathematical concepts)
- Verbal/linguistic (language in all its varied forms)
- Visual/spatial (visual data that may involve patterns, shapes, and drawings)
- Musical/rhythmical (rhythm, rhymes)
- Bodily/kinestethic (through movement and physical means)
- Interpersonal (interacting with others)
- Intrapersonal (thinking and self-reflection)
- Naturalistic (natural surroundings)

Rather than operating as separate entities, the intelligences almost always work synergistically as we learn and solve problems. In addition to these eight is *existential intelligence* (learning by questioning), which relates to a search for meaning. However, existential intelligence is not on Gardner's list yet, given that brain-based evidence for including this intelligence is inconclusive as of this writing.

To learn more about MI theory, be sure to read Howard Gardner's book, *Multiple Intelligences Go to School.* For ideas about how technology can be used in ways that support MI theory, see Annette Lamb's helpful suggestions on *Eduscape.com*.

Instead of trying to do justice to MI theory in this book, my goal is to underscore its relevance when developing ways to adapt new media to meet your learning objectives. After all, children come to school with abilities in each of the eight domains Gardner identified. Ultimately children need to be proficient in all of them to be accomplished readers and writers, and moreover, successful members of society.

Here's a case in point, involving Kristi Rennebohm Franz, a friend and colleague who drew upon MI theory in developing a curricular unit for her first- and second-graders in Pullman, Washington. Ms. Franz's goal was to create a global education unit about the environment beginning with a study of their local pond.[10] By observing the pond over time, children were able to collect data about the changes with time in the pond water's habitats—negative changes that raised environmental red flags. Students' findings motivated them to conduct additional research that extended far beyond their community. They consulted with government agencies and science experts via the Internet.

But what's particularly striking about Ms. Franz's approach is the way it reflected multiple intelligences theory. For example, some students created original artwork about the habitat while others collaborated on a mural. Children tapped into their interpersonal and linguistic intelligences to produce videos about the pond that they themselves had edited. Mathematical reasoning came into play when children counted species populations and learned how to use measurement tools. Children drew upon linguistic and interpersonal intelligences when they exchanged email messages, built a website, and videoconferenced with peers. Ultimately students reported what they had learned using traditional, real-time presentation skills. In brief, Ms. Franz developed a curriculum that reflects MI theory. As such, it offered children myriad ways to contribute to the habitat study.

NEW TECHNOLOGIES CAN BE COAXED TO HELP DEVELOP LITERACY SKILLS

I was curious to learn more about other teachers, who, like Ms. Franz, were trying to coax new tools to help children develop literacy skills. I decided to investigate further.

My search led me to a thirty-year veteran teacher named Martha Stackpole, from Martha's Vineyard, who uses telecommunication tools to help her children extend their reach beyond their island, a small gem several miles off the coast of Massachusetts. Having children compose, send, and receive messages aligns with Ms. Stackpole's larger goal of helping children become fluent readers and writers. In Ms. Stackpole's view, technology never drives the lesson; it's there as a way to, say, conduct biographical research for a multimedia report or create a website about the animal life found in a local saltwater pond.

I also learned from administrators. For example, Cheryl Forster, an award-winning middle school principal on Massachusetts' North Shore taught me how she gets her teachers onboard in regard to rethinking their literacy practices to take advantage of digital tools. She takes a direct approach, telling her faculty,

> The bus is leaving. Either you're getting on the bus, or it's pulling away from the curb. There's no choice any longer about whether or not you *can* or *should* be involved in technology. Clearly technology's here to stay. Ask yourself the question: Will there be more or less of it in five years? There will clearly be *more* of it in five years. And principals have a responsibility to make sure that in their leadership technology is a major piece. And that it affects curriculum, it affects school culture, it affects these skills that are, you know, the expanded version. Literacy is no longer very defined in microscopic terms. Literacy is now like this [throws out her arms in an expansive gesture]! (Fall, 2001)

Innovative educators amaze me. In interviewing dozens of them statewide, most seem surprised when I approached them about documenting their work. Ironically, as much as they enjoy touting their students' work they shy away from accolades about their own work. Fortunately, good teaching speaks for itself. One teacher showed me how she uses specially adapted keyboards to help her second-graders with motor difficulties learn to write. An eighth-grade LD teacher explained how she uses a camcorder to improve comprehension when teaching *Hamlet*. She has students write and dramatize skits, based on the play, and then film them. Composing and dramatizing the scenes helps students understand the literary elements of *Hamlet*. Replaying the taped versions of their skits helps kids get under the skin of the characters to figure out what makes them tick, thereby deepening their comprehension of the play.

Beyond Massachusetts, I've attended conferences on technology in education. One of the most memorable sessions involved English teachers from extremely isolated regions in America. These teachers set up a correspondence, via email, so students could discuss literature. One title they chose was Anne Frank's *Diary of a Young Girl*. Think of it. Students from the Mississippi Delta writing to peers in rural Alaska!

The exchange allowed them to share their common understandings of the literature; it also provided a forum for relating personal experience to literature—one that was shaped, in part, by local culture.[11]

Sometimes a forward-thinking teacher finds me. That's how I met Sandy Beck, a technology specialist from Georgia, who is interested in helping the teachers in her elementary school.[12] Sandy had read a paper I published on the Web about the marriage between computers and process writing. From Ms. Beck I learned what it's like to be a technology advocate within a school system that is on the cusp of change. Ms. Beck helped her teachers participate in a virtual adventure called "MayaQuest" through Classroom Connect. She also devised a way for teachers to create online student assessment portfolios, a method she presents at national conferences. Of Ms. Beck's commitment to children and technology, which often keeps her busy long after the school day, she remarked, "We live in the twenty-first century. This is what our kids deserve."[13]

I also learn from students by watching what happens when they get their hands on technology. What they decide to do with a digital camera, or electronic publishing tools, for example, is incredible. For example, MIT researcher Mitchell Resnick once invited children to invent a way to use new tools. One young girl responded by creating a print-based diary that used a high-tech lock to fend off prying eyes. Her diary also had a built-in camera to catch intruders red-handed. A pretty useful invention!

To learn from children in school settings, I spent nearly an entire school year perched on Lilliputian-sized chairs in local first- and second-grade classrooms. I got to watch as two boys, one American, the other a Korean who was just learning to speak English, created their own hypertext presentation about the Sonoran Desert. They were completely undaunted by the complexities of HyperStudio, a software tool that allows the user to build a set of hyperlinked texts, sounds, and images. The boys conducted research on cacti and desert animals with relative ease (their teacher had bookmarked relevant sites). So engrossed were they in their project that their conversation seldom veered off the topic at hand. Their final product consisted of only about four screens. Yet it was clear that the boys knew their stuff technologically speaking. It was also obvious that by conducting research and creating text, they had become experts on desert life.

In Boston's inner city, I've observed children as they invented simple machines and activities using the programming language LEGO/Logo, developed by Seymour Papert at MIT. Interestingly, the top students were not necessarily the best programmers. In fact, as teachers pointed out, some of the most avid LEGO/Logo users came from the lowest reading group. But they "got it" on a deeper level than many of their peers. (Incidentally, here's an example of multiple intelligences.)

My observations of children also moved beyond the classroom. For example I became a mentor at Boston's Computer Clubhouse. I've watched as girls, albeit tentatively, designed their own fashions, scanned in images, or recorded their original musical scores in the recording studio. I say tentatively, because when I first volunteered at the Clubhouse, the computers were dominated by boys. Fearless boys would fly airplanes (using software simulations, that is) and create animations while girls typically sat on the sidelines, tooling around at the edges of possibility. However, once the girls figured out how to advance their *own* agenda—which often involved communication, the arts, and fashion—they reached an important turning point. Eventually the girls, as a group, gained momentum. One of the most encouraging signs was the way they began to rely *on each other* to master more sophisticated applications.[14]

I stand in awe of all that I have witnessed, and wonder about the *many* other teachers who are creating a new world order. What strategies are they using to help their students become literate members of today's society?

WHAT DO KIDS REALLY NEED TO KNOW TO SUCCEED?

In today's world, becoming literate includes developing *technological fluency,* or the ability to mold and shape new tools for *one's own* educational purposes. It all hinges on this. To computer guru Seymour Papert of MIT, the term *technological fluency* refers to "the ability to use and apply technology in a fluent way, naturally and smoothly, as one does with language."[15] Take a spreadsheet, for example. Kids can create a spreadsheet that reads like a phone book. Or, they can figure out how to design a spreadsheet that helps them analyze real-world data, such as baseball scores or profits and losses from their own small-business ventures.

When students achieve technological fluency the world is their oyster! They can navigate their way through the surfeit of websites and other media that the information age has spawned. They can use word processing software to compose their ideas. They can exercise their critical thinking skills by evaluating information from different sources.

What is the teacher's role? One crisp New England afternoon I asked Kathleen O'Reilly, a third-grade teacher I visited at a school in Boston's North Shore, whether teaching literacy using new technologies was the same or different from traditional teaching. Ms. O'Reilly replied,

> I think it [teaching literacy] is a fundamentally different way to teach. They [students] think in different ways. The technology helps them think more logically; helps them solve their problems. When they encounter a problem on the computers I think they're a little more creative about how to solve it. And perhaps it's also our method of teaching; this school asks children to be *self-directed*. And I think the technology ties into that.

But does using new tools really alter a students' perspective psychologically and academically, I pressed? Ms. O'Reilly remarked,

> I think it [technology] really transforms the way they look at school, the way they're motivated to learn. I've seen it build confidence. There are kids who know exactly how to find a website that they need. Or to type a paragraph without having a kid sitting next to them. It has just really built their confidence. And I think the learning is more intense and rich. It's more practical. These are skills they can use in *a future that belongs to them*.[16]

I especially like Ms. O'Reilly's last statement. She is teaching her eight-year-olds how to be technologically fluent for "a future that belongs to them." Thanks to her and the other forward-thinking teachers I've had the good fortune to spend time with, many students are being offered the education they deserve. And ultimately we may achieve a much more equitable society than was possible in previous eras.

TAKING A STEP BACK TO CRITIQUE THE TEACHING PROFESSION

How can such fundamental changes take root within a field that is beset with problems (i.e., low salaries, lack of respect, few chances for upward mobility)? To truly understand how to use new tools for literacy instruction, we first need to reflect on the cultural context in which teaching takes place. We also need to acknowledge that teaching is a really, really tough job.

Research shows that teaching is an unsustainable profession. Fifty percent of teachers, who receive little collegial support, leave the profession after five years.[17] That's why we have so many new teachers who haven't had the benefit of intensive training and/or experience. To exacerbate the problem, novice teachers are often left to make it on their own once they've entered the classroom.[18] This practice would be unthinkable in most other professions, from becoming a barber, or chef, or a physician.

The attrition rates are especially alarming when you consider the Department of Education's estimate that our nation will need to hire *two million new qualified teachers* by the year 2010.[19] Where will we find them when so few college students are going into the field? And how well prepared will they be to teach reading and language arts? How will they address the fact that nearly 70 percent of all low-income fourth-graders are reading below grade level?[20] Finding developmentally appropriate materials for at-risk students that are written on their instructional levels is no easy task. (Later, in Part 2, I'll show you how technology can be a godsend in developing curricular materials for diverse learners.)

Yet, hope springs eternal. Many of today's idealistic young people *are* becoming teachers. With the future of eighty million young people in the balance, new teachers need whatever help we can give them. One of the best gifts we can offer is an understanding of how to use new tools to augment their efforts. If they're able to use technology well, especially to promote literacy, they may eventually draw deep satisfaction from their work and gain a sense of professionalism. Ideally, they'll decide to stay in the profession longer, lending their expertise to incoming novices.

"THE ODDS ARE SO AGAINST IT"

If you study the past
and use it to understand the present
then you're worthy to be a teacher.
                            —CONFUCIUS

I was in a frame of mind to mull over these issues one evening when I attended a talk presented by David McCullough, the Pulitzer Prize–winning author of the best-selling biography of John Adams.[21] One of the most compelling facets of the talk was McCullough's description of what it was like to be alive during John Adams' era—the eighteenth century. The better we understand the historical context, the author pointed out, the better we can understand Adams—his ambitions, and the dilemmas he faced in achieving them. First, McCullough advised, we need to try to scale down the world. We need to envision the smallness of Boston with its population of a mere 15,000 people. The largest city, Philadelphia, in which delegates attended the First Continental Congress in 1774, had a population of only 30,000. Leon Eisenberg, Communications Secretary of the American Academy of Arts and Sciences, later summarized McCullough's words:

> The people who assembled in Philadelphia were scholar-patriots, brand new to the idea of a revolution. If a poll had been taken in the Colonies in that year, they would have scrapped the whole idea. Perhaps a third favored it, a third were against it, and the others were waiting to see which way the wind blew. But they persisted. They weren't demigods. Every one of them had his flaws, failings, and weaknesses. The miracle is that these imperfect human beings, with all the difficulties of just getting through a day in the 18th century, rose to the occasion. The more one reads about the Declaration of Independence and the first ten to twelve years after the war, the more one has to feel how incredible it is that it ever happened, the odds were so against it. (p. 2)

McCullough's words were not only stirring. In an indirect way they helped me to understand the radical shifts taking place in today's schools. I thought about the Founding Fathers and the overwhelming odds *they* faced, and found a parallel with today's teachers and their technological revolution. Think of the overwhelming odds teachers face. As with the American Revolution, it's incredible that this twenty-first-century revolution is taking place in schools at all. The odds are nearly as stacked against schools having the know-how and equipment as they were against our becoming "a nation unto itself" so many years ago.

YOUTH CULTURE

While change in colonial days was largely due to the hard work and foresight of the Founding Fathers, change today often comes about not only through teachers' hard work but because young people demand it. Students are often better connected, electronically, than their elders. They're also more adventurous in the way they approach new tools. They bring excitement, confidence, and enthusiasm to new challenges involving media that leave older generations profoundly perplexed.

One aspect of youth culture, related to literacy, is the instant messaging (IM) phenomenon. Nearly 60 percent of students who have access to telecommunication tools engage in instant messaging, according to Nielsen/NetRatings.[22] Students use IM to socialize, collaborate on homework, make dates, and so on. Who would have guessed that adolescents would choose to write messages as a primary way to connect with friends, right up there with talking in person? In fact, some say it's possible that adolescents spend as much time writing to each other as they spend on formal writing assignments. And because IM has evolved as an integral part of youth culture, it has spawned its own vocabulary (*u, ur, b4, wuz,* and *cuz*) that often leaves adults bewildered, or at least bemused.[23]

Students who are hooked on instant messaging are part of a new society of children, ages eight and older, who on average spend six and three-quarter hours a day—outside of school—engaged with some form of media, from books, to television, to CD-ROMs, to Game Boy™. These findings were revealed by a Kaiser Family Foundation national study of over 3,000 children and adolescents. Within this group, over two-thirds have televisions in their bedrooms; nearly half eat meals in front of the television.[24] Children in the younger group (ages two through seven) typically spend three and one-half hours per day involved with various media.

This brings to mind Peter Holtz, a middle school teacher in Ipswich, Massachusetts, who is keenly aware of how well his students understand the possibilities of new tools. When I visited his school Mr. Holtz remarked, "Rather than the teacher saying 'We want you to do this, what they [his students] say is '*Can* we do this? *Can* we do that?' Because they have Publisher under their belts from past years,

Open-ended Tools for Digital Publishing: Thumbnail Sketches

PowerPoint, Microsoft

Arguably the most popular presentation software product, originally designed for adults but appropriated by students as young as eight years old. Built-in "wizards" offer templates for putting together multimedia presentations. PowerPoint can be purchased separately or as part of Microsoft Office Suite.

Microsoft Publisher, Microsoft

Although developed for business applications, many adolescents find Publisher a powerful tool for creating newsletters, flyers, and CD jackets.

EasyBook Deluxe, Sunburst Communications

Students can design their own illustrated publications and print them in several formats, such as minibooks and poster-sized books. Features include a spell-checker, thesaurus, and drawing tools. The text-to-speech feature is especially beneficial, as it lets students hear their books read aloud.

HyperStudio, Knowledge Adventure

A creativity tool that simplifies the process of creating multimedia presentations. Students can import sounds, animations, and videos into their reports and other projects. Art tools are included via pull-down menus.

Inspiration, Inspiration, Inc.

An inspired product, Inspiration allows children to map out their ideas in the form of graphic organizers. Once they've created their graphic organizers, or built one using a template, students can, with a single click, view their ideas in outline format. See also Kidspiration, a simpler, more graphic version designed for primary-grade students.

Amazing Writing Machine, Broderbund (The Learning Company)

An electronic writing center for students that offers story starters and templates for writing in multiple genres (e.g., letter writing, poetry, and journals). The drawing tools are from the popular KidPix product. Students can hear their compositions read back by one of eight synthesized voices.

and [proficiency in] PowerPoint, they can do it. It's a great motivator. Kids are in the driver's seat."[25]

BUT CAN COMPUTERS REALLY MAKE YOU SMARTER?

A tool is not just a tool is a tool any more than a rose is just a rose is a rose, to paraphrase Gertrude Stein shamelessly. The Russian philosopher, Lev Vygotsky, believed that tools have a profound influence on our development; tools mediate the human experience.[26]

What are the implications for literacy learning? Take the popular application PowerPoint for example. Whenever I create a PowerPoint presentation I think of writer Ian Parker's scathing critique in an article that appeared in *The New Yorker*.[27] PowerPoint is anything but neutral, Parker maintains. It tries to control our thinking in subtle ways. It edits our ideas, with a very heavy hand that often changes the nature of our message.

If you've ever tried to use a PowerPoint's wizard to help you create a presentation, you too may have felt you were forced to toe the line. No long paragraphs allowed! In fact, all text needs to be formatted as bullet points, and only a limited number of points at that. Yet, an estimated 30 million PowerPoint presentations are being made each day, according to Microsoft.[28] Given its wide acceptance, I think it's fair to say that this tool has had an enormous impact on the way we express our ideas and communicate them to others.

FROM PAST TO PRESENT

The idea of tools as nonneutral objects that are capable of influencing our thinking is not new. At the turn of the twentieth century, John Dewey gave careful consideration to tools as objects that can reveal larger worlds to us. Dewey believed that the essential purpose of tools is to permit larger ideas to surface.[29] If we teach students to weave, to draw upon a classic Deweyan example, it's not just because we want them to learn to make woolen cloth. The larger idea is that after students master the skills it takes to weave cloth, they can better understand the modern loom. Dewey claims that wisdom comes from "working it out experimentally, thus seeing its

necessity, and tracing its effects, not only upon that particular industry, but upon modes of social life"[30] To Dewey's thinking, tools *reveal* larger worlds to us. Everyday technologies can *disclose* information. Within a Deweyan framework, then, we need to use tools to lend new meaning to our everyday lives, by helping us perceive larger worlds—worlds students can add their imprimatur to through reading and writing.

A RUSSIAN PHILOSOPHER AND THE ZONE OF PROXIMAL DEVELOPMENT

Writing tools also allow us to work in what Vygotsky called our Zone of Proximal Development, or ZPD.[31] When working in the ZPD, learning is supported, or scaffolded, in ways that allow children to perform at a higher level than if they were working without them, as though they were working with a mentor. A classic example of how the ZPD works is the game of tennis. If you want to become a better tennis player, you'd be smart to select an opponent who is a stronger player than you are, so you can rise to his or her level. Similarly, Vygotsky believed that children who receive support, *within an apprenticeship model*, often realize higher goals that they would on their own.

It's also true that learning to use tools helps children develop an understanding of the signs of the culture, or language use. A first-grader who composes with an adult, using a word processor, can often create a more sophisticated big book than she could if using paper and pencil. You can input the child's verbal constructions, engage her in discussions of punctuation, word choice, plot, character development, and so on, with one important difference: The text appears on a computer monitor in 24-point type right before her eyes. Thus children can effectively interact with their own written words in a way that's more dynamic than would be possible with pencil and paper. You can ask questions such as, "What you just said sounds like a conversation between two characters. What type of punctuation do we need?" and so on.

IMPLICATIONS FOR YOUR TEACHING

Can we really compare innovative teachers of reading and writing in twenty-first-century schools with the efforts of the Founding Fathers? I think so. People in both historical eras have sought a new path toward a learned and democratic society. Leaders in both eras have been revolutionary in their thinking.

If you're one of the legion of teachers whose classroom is wired, and you want to know more about what children can actually do in cyberspace to promote literacy, the next three chapters can help you. They'll show you how and where to begin—and ultimately, how you can maximize your efforts to help *all* your students become literate members of the digital age.

ENDNOTES

1. Milton Chen, *Edutopia* (San Francisco: Jossey-Bass, 2002), 117.
2. Alan Collins, "Wither Technology and Schools?" In C. Fisher, D. C. Dwyer, K. Yocam (eds.). *Education and Technology: Reflections on Computing in Classrooms.* (San Francisco: Jossey-Bass, 1996).
3. Lawrence Cuban, *Teachers and Machines: The Classroom Use of Technology Since 1920.* (New York: Teachers College Press, 1986). Also, Fisher, C. Learning to Compute and Computing to Learn. In C. Fisher, D. C. Dwyer, K. Yocam (eds.), *Education and Technology: Reflections on Computing in Classrooms.* (San Francisco: Jossey-Bass, 1996).
4. Lawrence Cuban, *Oversold and Underused.* (Cambridge, MA: Harvard University Press, 2001), 195.
5. This section is drawn from my unpublished doctoral thesis, Early Literacy Instruction and Educational Technologies, (Cambridge, MA: Harvard Graduate School of Education, 1999), 187.
6. Rebecca Paula Pierik, "Beyond the Divide." *Ed.: The Magazine of the Harvard Graduate School of Education.* Vol. XLVII, No. 1, Spring 2003, 14.
7. All URLs mentioned in this book were valid at the time of publication.
8. Sandy Beck's website: *www.forsyth.k12.ga.us/sbeck/teacher_making_the_connection5.htm.)*

9. Howard Gardner, *Intelligence Reframed: Multiple Intelligences for the 21st Century* (New York: Basic Books, 2000).

10. Kristi Rennebohm Franz's case study: *learnweb.harvard.edu/ent /gallery/ pop3/pop3_1.cfm*. (*Note:* This Picture of Practice of Kristi and her students also offers a case study of the Teaching for Understanding technique described in Part 3.)

11. For a more detailed account see: Scott Christian, *Exchanging Lives. Middle School Writers Online.* (Urbana, Ill: National Council of Teachers of English, 1997).

12. For an interview with Sandy Beck, Jon Scieszka, and myself see *Teacher.Radio.com* at Scholastic. URL: *teacher.scholastic.com/professional/ techexpert/forum.asp*

13. Interview notes, April 19, 2001.

14. One of the best resources for gaining insight into the gender gap and technology is *Tech Savvy*, a report published by the American Association of University Women, Washington, D.C.

15. See reference to Seymour Papert's discussion of "technological fluency" at *web.media.mit.edu/~calla/web_comunidad/seminar.htm*

16. Interview notes, Fall, 2002.

17. Milton Chen (ed.) (2002), *Edutopia.*

18. Vivian Troen and Katherine C. Boles, *Who's teaching your children?* (New Haven: Yale University Press, 2003), 15.

19. Milton Chen (ed.) *Edutopia.* (San Francisco: Jossey-Bass, 2002), 234.

20. Strauss, V. (2002, September 15). "Educators say Bush pushing commercial phonics products." *The Boston Globe*, A22.

21. McCullough's talk was called "John Adams and the Good Life of the Mind." It was delivered at the American Academy of Arts & Sciences and the Boston Athenaeum, March 13, 2002, Memorial Chapel, Harvard University. While writing this passage I discovered that this book earned the author a second Pulitzer Prize!

22. Lee, J. (2002, September 19). "I Think, Therefore IM" *The New York Times*, pp. E1 and E4.

23. *ibid.*, p. E1.

24. J. Kiesewetter, and C. Kranz, (1999, November 18). "Media Has Big Influence on Kids," *Cincinnati Enquirer* (web edition: *www.enquirer.com/ editions/1999/11/18/loc_media_has_big.html*).

25. Interview with Peter Holtz on April 23, 2001.

26. James V. Wertsch, *A Sociocultural Approach to Mind: Child Development Today and Tomorrow*. (San Francisco: Jossey-Bass, 1989).

27. Ian Parker (May 28, 2001). "Absolute PowerPoint." In *The New Yorker*, 2001, May 28, 76–87.

28. Ian Parker, op. cit.

29. David Blacker, "Allowing Educational Technologies to Reveal: A Deweyan Perspective." *Educational Theory*, Vol. 43, No. 2, Spring, 1993.

30. 1899, p. 13, 92; cited in Blacker, 1993, 191.

31. L. S. Vygotsky, *Mind in Society*, (Cambridge, MA: Harvard University Press, 1978; Original work published in 1934).

2

PART

Seven Ways to Use New Media to Improve Reading and Writing Instruction

Literacy is inseparable from opportunity, and opportunity is inseparable from freedom. The freedom promised by literacy is both freedom from—from ignorance, oppression, poverty—and freedom to—to do new things, to make choices, to learn.

—Koïchiro Matsuura, UNESCO Director General

If you're reading this book, you are probably concerned about the children you're working with who are falling behind as readers and writers. The students who concern you most may have been diagnosed as learning disabled, dyslexic, and/or attention deficit disordered (ADD). They may have simply missed out on schooling because of frequent absences. Or, they may be English Language Learners, strong students in their native languages but faltering in English-only classrooms.

Literacy experts Chall and Popp summarize why many children of average and above-average intelligence have difficulty learning to read, as follows.

> Over the past century, psychologists, neurologists, psychiatrists, and educators have proposed various reasons. Some focused on poor teaching, while others sought answers in the social, psychological, and medical areas. The prevailing views on causation include neurological explanations (that reading disability stems from difference in the brain), educational explanations (that reading failure is caused by inadequate

reading instructional methods), and social and emotional explanations (that reading problems come from the individual's social background and/or emotional problems). Increasingly, from about the 1960s, reading difficulties have been viewed by many as stemming from neurological factors, but one or more of the above causes may help explain an individual's reading problem; therefore, those with severe problems in learning to read should be referred for a comprehensive diagnosis.[1]

Once your struggling readers have been diagnosed by a team of experts, they'll need to receive carefully targeted instruction as soon as possible. But even with extra help, catching up is hard to do. Research shows that below-average readers need to make *even more than one year's growth* in reading during the school year to draw even with the gains average learners make during a school year.

Fortunately, the digital age has brought us tools that can enhance a balanced approach to literacy learning. In Part 2, I will describe ways to use new tools in support of seven essential literacy practices:

- Word recognition
- Fluency
- Comprehension
- Vocabulary
- Reading and writing across the curriculum
- Process writing
- Motivation

I hope that the strategies I present in this section will give you a chance to reflect on your teaching style and how you might extend your current repertoire. When it comes to helping every one of our students become accomplished readers and writers, we need to take full advantage of every conceivable tool for learning.

ESSENTIAL LITERACY PRACTICE 1: WORD RECOGNITION

Experts recommend that teachers provide direct, systematic instruction in word recognition skills. How can you use new media—computers and educational television, for example—to help students practice their emerging skills in a variety of interesting contexts?

*Collectively these studies [all reading research up until the late 1980s]
suggest, with impressive consistency, that programs including systematic
instruction on letter-to-sound correspondences lead to higher achievement in
both word recognition and spelling, at least in the early grades and especially
for slower or economically disadvantaged students.*
—Marilyn Jager Adams[2]

Why Do Some Children Struggle with Word Recognition?

Good readers can decode unfamiliar words because they understand
the relationship between sounds, the letters that stand for sounds, and
how to blend sounds together to make words. Poor readers, in contrast,
who have not broken the alphabetic code will experience tremendous
difficulty in learning to read no matter how motivated they are, and no
matter how stimulating the classroom climate.

Good readers are also able to recognize *sight words,* or common
everyday words that often are phonetically irregular (for example,
enough, which, and *friend*) automatically. Sight words are particularly
important because they pop up everywhere; they are the mortar that
holds together the building blocks of English. Thus, instant recognition
of sight words is a precursor for fluent reading.

Despite the cognitive demands experienced in learning to read,
many children learn to read quite young, even before entering kindergarten. But with other students, especially those in underserved populations, it takes longer. In addition, many students who experience
difficulty in decoding unfamiliar words are learning disabled. The
source of their difficulty is often related to *developmental dyslexia,* a disorder that we have learned more about in recent years because of
advances in brain research, specifically, the use of sophisticated imag-
ining techniques. Since the 1990s an imaging technique called func-
tional magnetic resonance imaging (fMRI) has made the brain "trans-
parent"; researchers can track where a "glucose burn" (brain activity)
occurs during particular tasks such as decoding or adding numbers.[3]
With this type of dyslexia, students have tremendous difficulty decoding at the single word level, which impedes their ability to read quickly
or fluently. This is especially puzzling because research shows that
students who are affected by developmental dyslexia typically have
average or above-average intelligence. Some may be gifted.[4]

Symptoms of developmental dyslexia can include the following. First-graders may still have difficulty recognizing and manipulating phonemes, reading common one-syllable words such as *mat* or *top*, and learning sight words such as *said*, *where*, and *two*. With older children, symptoms may include: mispronouncing long or complicated words; confusing words that sound alike such as *margin* and *margarine*; memorizing dates, names, and telephone numbers; applying decoding skills to multisyllabic words rather than guessing; difficulty completing homework and/or tests on time; and an aversion to reading aloud.[5] If you suspect one of your students is affected by developmental dyslexia, it's best to refer him or her for a thorough evaluation as soon as possible to determine a course of action.

Websites That Promote Phonemic Analysis and Phonics Skills

For Games that focus on phonemic analysis, see PBS's *Between the Lions* website. Among the many excellent activities, be sure to see Fuzzy Ears and Pounce (*pbskids.org/lions/*). For practice in phonics, see Clifford's Sound Match, which emphasizes beginning sounds in words. See *teacher.scholastic.com/clifford1/flash/phonics/index.htm*. More advanced readers might enjoy Marvin Morrison's Word Puzzles for additional practice in phonics. (See *www.soundpuzzle.com/index.html*)

How New Technologies Can Help Your Students Develop Word Recognition Skills

Practice is an essential component of learning to apply word recognition skills to unfamiliar words. The new brain imaging techniques described previously confirm that practice has a positive effect on developing expertise, even with children as young as four and five years old. Through practice, the brain creates the type of neural circuits that are necessary to read well.[6]

Software products can provide a stimulating way for children to get the practice they need in these ways.

1. Students can repeat challenging activities as often as necessary.
2. Students can make mistakes in front of the computer without embarrassment.
3. The computer offers children multimodal experiences in learning to recognize words, which benefits all types of learners. A child can *see* the word (*visual*), *hear* it read aloud in isolation and in sentences (*auditory*), *type* in letters to create words (*kinesthetic*), *say* the word to the computer, and *listen* to it as it is read back (*verbal and auditory*).

Software products that take advantages of the full potential of new media are the ones you want to invest in. Look for those that offer students ways to customize instruction, draw upon several of their senses, and practice in lively and engaging formats. Products to avoid include those that rely heavily on lackluster drill-and-practice routine—ones that seldom invite students to apply skills to *actually reading connected text.* What good is it, you might ask, to have children click on virtual eggs to make words like *hen, pen,* and *ten,* if they never get to practice reading these words in a story about a hen?

The question of what makes a software product good, or very good, is one that has intrigued me for many years. I've decided that it's pretty hard to pin down. We all recognize low-quality software when we see it, with its stereotypical treatment of females and/or people of color, its superficial activities, and over-the-top graphics. But what about all the software products that are really quite good? How do you decide which to use in your school?

One big question to ask yourself is whether the software product stimulates children's thinking in ways that go far beyond drill and practice routines. Does it *empower* them, by allowing them to build or create something original and worthwhile that would have been nearly impossible otherwise?

In developing guidelines for evaluating software, I drew upon the work of technology integration experts Barbara Means, William Peneul, and Christine Padilla, authors of *The Connected School,* who first opened my eyes to the importance of student empowerment as the main criterion.[7] If our agenda is to use software as one way to level the playing field, then children in poorer districts should have opportunities to use the sorts of mind-expanding tools that children in more affluent districts use routinely.

Here are several guidelines to help you evaluate software for your unique learning environment.

Guidelines for Student-empowered Technology Use

Does the particular piece of software (or website) support student-empowered literacy learning? Specifically, does it:

1. Emulate the ways in which professional readers, writers, and communicators use technology?
2. Involve complex tasks, such as conducting research, summarizing findings using one's own words, and presenting information?
3. Require significant amounts of time for completion, as with online journals and collaborative writing projects?
4. Give students latitude in designing their own products and in determining when and how to use technology in reading and language arts?
5. Involve multiple academic disciplines, as in extending literacy skills across science, social studies, and math?
6. Provide opportunities for student collaboration with peers and outside experts in ways that incorporate authentic reading and writing tasks?

If we take criterion one, certainly open-ended writing and publishing tools emulate the way professionals work. Many of these same tools, such as PowerPoint, provide a structure that supports students in creating presentations based on their research. As for criterion three, most truly worthwhile projects really do need time to germinate. After all, most real learning takes place not in a single episode, but over several weeks or months. A drill and practice matching or sorting game that's over in ten minutes can carry a student only so far up the learning curve. Criterion four speaks to critical thinking skills as they apply to new technologies. That is, determining which literacy tools to use for which intellectual purpose is a life skill. We need to help students become confident enough to make their own decisions. Fifth, software can help students build bridges across curricular areas; charts, graphs, and databases can all be integrated into science and social studies curricula to deepen students' understanding of a topic or event. And sixth, student collaborations that involve peers and/or transcend classroom walls can broaden a student's world view in ways that weren't remotely possible before the advent of modern telecommunications tools.

Do these criteria align with the guidelines you've been using? What ways have you found to foster student empowerment using new tools? These questions could be the beginning of a great discussion with your colleagues.

Photography in the Classroom

Using photography to enhance literacy learning is infinitely more possible today than ever before. Cameras have become relatively inexpensive, especially disposable 35-millimeter cameras and low-end digital cameras. The potential is enormous. Young children can create photo journals by taking pictures that correspond with target sounds. For example, a search for -ake family words could lead to photos depicting *take, make, rake, lake, stake,* and so on. Have students practice reading and writing target words by creating individual photo journals, or collecting words in a class book. Then ask children to create a caption for each photo. (Did you know that you can have 35-mm film developed and converted to digital images, which makes importing them into word processing software a breeze?) Older students can create more sophisticated photo journals featuring more challenging, multisyllabic words.

Or, they can act out synonyms and antonyms (e.g., *ecstatic/melancholy*) and create a class ebook to display their work. For inspiration, see the Polaroid Education Program's website, which documents ideas from teachers (*www.polaroid.com*). You can also order Polaroid's free Visual Learning Guide, one of which is focused on special education needs, and find out how to apply for a grant.

Software to Support Phonics Instruction

Destination Reading Series, Riverdeep, is a software program that was developed in collaboration with national reading experts. The software carefully sequences skills so each one of them serves as a building block for the next. Phonics is one of the blocks, along with vocabulary, comprehension, and others. (See *Riverdeep.net*)

Clifford Reading, Scholastic, for ages four through six. The popular animated dog, Clifford, entices children to interact with a systematic approach to phonics; varying degrees of challenge are built into the product. (See *www.scholastic.com*)

Arthur (Various titles, such as "Wilderness Adventure" and "Space-Flyers Alien Space Chase"), Broderbund. Arthur, the animated star of the popular PBS series with the same name, leads young learners through imaginative adventures to help build and solidify phonics skills. (See *Broderbund.com*)

Tenth Planet Literacy Series, Sunburst. Letter sounds, long and short vowels—these are just a few of the skills children can practice by interacting with this software product that combines heavy doses of humor with activities that really cause young children to think. (See *Sunburst.com*)

Daisy Quest and Daisy's Castle, Adventure Learning Software. Three engaging adventures are included on one CD-ROM designed to help students develop phonological awareness (e.g., rhyming, beginning and ending sounds in words, and word blending). Online evaluation tools included. (See *www.acciinc.com/software/daisy_quest.htm*)

Educational Television

Sesame Street, produced by the Public Broadcasting System. How many of you came of age under Big Bird's big yellow wing? *Sesame Street* is still going strong after all these years with additional features such as Spanish language components and Web activities that enhance the TV program. (Check local listings; for Web activities see *www.pbskids.org/sesame/*)

Between the Lions, coproduced by WGBH (Boston's public television station) and Thinking, Ltd., of New York. Designed for children ages four through seven, the TV show also invites parents to be coviewers. Award-winning children's literature is the focus of a lion family that lives—where else?—in a public library. Hilarious animated characters such as Chicken Jane and Cliff Hanger star in skits that reinforce word recognition skills.

Enhancing Your Word Recognition Program with Technology

In addition to discovering innovative ways to use photography, you can help students develop their word recognition skills by incorporating software products and educational television, as noted in the previous box.

Once children have developed their word recognition skills, typically by the end of first grade or early second grade, they'll be ready to work on becoming fluent readers. In terms of Chall's stages of reading development (more on this in Part 3), fluent reading typically begins in Stage 2, the "confirmation fluency and ungluing from print stage."[8]

ESSENTIAL LITERACY PRACTICE 2: FLUENCY

Why is fluency so important that it has become part of the national educational agenda? How can you help *all* students become fluent readers? How can you use computers as allies?

It is books that are a key to the wide world; if you can't do anything else, read all that you can.

—Jane Hamilton

In recent years, the realization that to be *proficient* readers children need to first become *fluent* readers has risen to the top of the national agenda. What does it mean to be a fluent reader? Fluent readers are able to read quickly and easily enough to focus active attention on meaning. You can measure reading fluency by determining the rate at which students can read aloud accurately and with prosody (proper expression).

What is the most effective way for you to help children become fluent readers? The message from the field, based on research, is loud and clear. *Guided oral reading practice* is the single best strategy for improving students' ability to read fluently. When children read and reread aloud regularly to a parent, sibling, or teacher, it has a positive effect on their reading fluency, which in turn leads to greater comprehension. An added bonus is that gains in these key areas often translate into gains in full-scale reading scores.

How should you go about providing guided oral reading practice? This technique can take the form of echo reading (in which readers closely "echo" the oral reading of a proficient reader), repeated reading (of the same text), shared reading (as in, you read one paragraph and I'll read one paragraph), choral reading (as in reading poetry as part of a group, paying particular attention to rhymes and rhythms), and other time-honored techniques. In any case, when a more capable reader provides one-on-one support *when needed*, children can make strong, reliable gains in fluency.[9]

Why Many Students Struggle with Reading Fluently

To read fluently, students need to recognize words rapidly (or even automatically) *and* understand what they read. This means they need to be able to apply their word recognition skills to decoding unfamiliar words. Students also need to have a well-developed vocabulary to draw upon when they encounter seldom-used words.

Unfortunately, for many students reading aloud is a painful process characterized by frequent pauses, self-corrections, and word substitutions. From their point of view, reading is too painful a task to be meaningful, and it certainly isn't fun.

Fluency expert Tim Rasinski offers this glimpse inside the mind of a disfluent reader:

> Imagine yourself as a fifth grade student who is assigned to read a twelve-page chapter in a social studies book in school. Imagine also

that you are a disfluent or inefficient reader. You read at fifty-eight words per minute. . . or half the rate of your classmates. You begin reading as best you can. Like most students you are well aware of what is happening around you. You are about halfway through the passage, and you notice that many of your classmates have finished reading— they are done and you still have six pages to read. What do you do? Do you pretend to have completed the assignment even though you haven't read or comprehended the entire passage? Or do you continue reading knowing that by doing so you will be broadcasting your lack of reading proficiency and making your classmates wait on you? Neither solution is palatable, yet the problem is all too common. . . Even if an assignment were made for home reading, the sixty-minute reading assignment for most students would become two hours of reading for you.[10]

No wonder disfluent readers often give up. But without practice, how will they ever become confident, proficient, fluent readers? Read on.

Reading Fluency

More fluent readers. . .
Are able to focus on comprehension. They focus their attention on making connections among the ideas in a text and between these ideas and their background knowledge.

Less fluent readers. . .
Must focus their attention primarily on decoding individual words. Therefore, they have little attention left for comprehending the text.[11]

Norms for Calibrating Students' Guided Reading Fluency

What are the average oral reading fluency rates for students at various times of year, at different grade levels, considered to be? Reading researchers such as Hasbrouck and Tindall[12] and companies such as Lexia have established national oral fluency norms. You can take advantage of these norms to look up data for the grade levels that interest you, at particular points during a school year. The Edformation website, for example, provides data collected from thousands of students, during the 2002–2003 school year (*www.edformation.com/norms.htm*). The norms have been calculated for the number of correct words read per minute (CWPM), counting these mistakes as errors: mispronunciations, substitutions, omissions, and hesitations lasting longer than three seconds.[13] You can follow these same guidelines, testing your students individually, for one minute, using a grade-level passage (containing at least 200 words) that they have never read. You'll also need to check for comprehension by asking a few questions about the passage after a child has read it.

An amazing feature of these one-minute timed tests is their high correlation with standardized tests that take *much* longer to administer, such as the Stanford Diagnostic Reading Test (word identification section) and the Woodcock Reading Master Test; in both cases the correlation is 0.94.[14] Thus, these timed tests can help you calibrate your students' progress with peers across the country. (For more detailed information and grade-level reading samples, I highly recommend Wiley Blevins' book, *Building Fluency*, 2001, available through Scholastic, Inc.)

Oral Reading Fluency Norms, Grades 2–5 (Hasbrouck and Tindall, 1992)

GRADE	PERCENTILE	CWPM FALL	CWPM WINTER	CWPM SPRING
2	75th	82	106	124
	50th	53	78	94
	25th	23	46	65
3	75th	107	123	142
	50th	79	93	114
	25th	65	70	87
4	75th	125	133	143
	50th	99	112	118
	25th	72	89	92
5	75th	126	143	151
	50th	105	118	128
	25th	77	93	100

Analysis of the CWPM rates at various grade levels sheds light on student progress nationally. You can see, for example:

- A strong reader (in the 75th percentile), at the end of the second grade, reads at 124 CWPM, on average.

- An average third-grader (50th percentile), midyear, reads 93 CWPM, on average.
- A low-achieving fifth-grader (in the 25th percentile) reads 77 CWPM, on average, in the fall. Most likely he or she has difficulty comprehending text.

These CWPM scores help us understand why children who read fluently read often, perhaps reading more words in a typical two-week period than a below-average reader does during an entire school year.[15] CWPM scores also offer us red flags, indicating which students need to receive intensive instruction.

How Can We Increase Fluency?

Not surprisingly, students need a great deal of practice in reading words correctly, over and over. Once new words have been mastered, children can add them to their sight vocabulary. At this stage, the child has built a mental model that will become more complete, helping him to recognize and understand it easily on the page.[16]

Researchers Stahl, Heubach, and Cramond suggest ideal practice conditions for increased oral reading fluency, which I have adapted below.[17]

Five Guidelines for Increasing Fluency

- Lessons should emphasize comprehension, even when smooth and fluent oral reading is the focus, so that children are always aware of the importance of understanding what they read.
- Children should read as many texts at their "comfort level" as possible—not too easy, not frustrating.
- Children need help when they engage in repeated readings of a given text until they can read it fluently.
- Children should have the opportunity to read with partners as a way to increase the amount of time they spend reading in school.
- Children should increase the time they spend reading at home.[18]

How Can You Use Technology to Help Your Students Become Fluent Readers?

The evidence is clear. Students need to engage in guided oral reading *often*, and their progress should be monitored. Yet even the most well-organized teacher would find it challenging to provide individual students with as much guided practice as they need. The numbers are against it: one teacher to twenty-plus students!

Computer software can help. For example, Soliloquy Learning's Reading Assistant helps children by inviting them to read selections into the computer.[19] By taking advantage of speech recognition technology, we can effectively "give the computer ears," to quote Marilyn J. Adams, Chief Scientist at Soliloquy Learning. That is, the computer can "listen" to a student as he reads into a microphone, and intervene when he needs help. For example, if a child hesitates for more than a predetermined number of seconds, or substitutes a word or phrase, the computer helps him. In addition to providing a virtual guided reading experience, the software also offers an online thesaurus, quizzes, and teacher management tools. Children can practice reading aloud in many different genres. Selections, which are largely drawn from *Cricket* and *Ladybug* magazines, as well as books about heroes (Lerner Publications), include plays, folktales, and contemporary fiction. In sum, the software can amplify your ability to give guided oral reading practice to all students. In classrooms that are equipped with three or four computers, it's not inconceivable that students could practice reading fluently for, say, a few twenty-minute sessions per week.

Similarly, Read Naturally offers students a carefully calibrated system for practicing oral reading fluency. Using audiocassettes or CD-ROMs, children can read and reread nonfiction passages as they listen to them being read aloud. A distinguishing feature of this product is that children are encouraged to create graphs to document their progress on each of the selections. This practice allows them to monitor their progress over time.

Just ten minutes a day of guided oral reading practice can address Stahl et al.'s guidelines and contribute importantly to children's ability to read fluently, with expression, and with an understanding of what they read. (Of course, twenty minutes of practice a day would be even better!)[20]

In addition to these software products, you might also set up a listening center in your classroom. That way students can read along as authors and/or actors model fluent, expressive reading. Many publishers offer audiobooks of popular titles for children and adolescents; some even come with tips for developing comprehension. Imagine a listening center in which students could read along as they listen to books such as *Favorite Greek Myths,* by Mary Pope Osborne, *Jonah the Whale,* by Susan Shreve, or *Pacific Crossing,* by Gary Soto (all published by Scholastic, Inc).[21] Also, check out Westin Woods in Norwalk, Connecticut, Recorded Books in Prince Frederick, Maryland, and Spoken Arts in New Rochelle, New York for additional titles.

Digital Tools to Help Build Fluency

What software products are available for developing fluency? Here are a few of the best.

Reading Assistant, Soliloquy Learning. Guided oral reading practice is enhanced through speech recognition technology as students read poems, adventures, and informational articles. (See *www.reading-assistant.com*)

Read Naturally offers readers practice through audiotapes and CD-ROMs. Children read a story aloud three or four times as they listen to it being read, and graph their progress. A Spanish language version is also available. (See *www.readnaturally.com*)

Great Leaps Reading is a print series that offers students five to six minutes of fluency practice a day. The texts are specifically targeted toward older children with reading difficulties. (See *www.greatleaps.com*)

Add a Little Drama with Readers' Theatre

Another popular activity to motivate students who struggle with oral reading fluency is Readers' Theatre. This technique focuses on the basics—reading and rereading with expression. Costumes, scenery, props, makeup, or even a stage are all optional. Your students will probably find it hard to resist the allure of dramatizing a scene from literature. Once they become excited about the idea of performing, they'll want to rehearse by reading the same parts over and over again so they'll sound polished when reading in front of their peers.

Children's librarian Esmé Raji Codell suggests that you begin by selecting a popular story that offers several enticing characters and dialog. Then create roles for actors, add a narrator and a few stage directions, and you're good to go.[22]

New media can add important dimensions to your productions, beyond offering an added incentive for students who have a flair for drama and/or directing a story. For older students, a unit on Shakespeare might fit in well with your curricula. The Internet can help you before you begin by providing free study guides for plays. The award-ing-winning website, "Mr. William Shakespeare and the Internet," for example, can save you hours of work, with its free downloads and links to especially pertinent resources (e.g., Shakespeare's life) that can breathe new life into your study of the bard. (See *shakespeare.palo-mar.edu/sitemap.htm*)

For younger students, the Internet is packed with free stories that your students can transform into scripts. Or, if you prefer to begin with ready-made scripts, you can find them for stories such as "How Frog Went to Heaven," "The Princess Mouse," and "Casey at the Bat." These scripts can lead to greater insights into characterization (which influ-ences how a character would deliver a particular line), plot structure (through a study of acts and scenes), and vocabulary (both the pronun-ciation of words and their nuanced meanings).

Beyond the Internet, you can capture students' performances by tak-ing digital photos of particular scenes for a class display or scrapbook, or by having students record them with camcorders. Either way, you can showcase student talent by posting projects to your school's web-site (using only students' first names for safety reasons).

A-Plus *Resources for Readers' Theatre*

Aaron Shepard's Reading Theatre

I would love to meet Mr. Shepard some day. He is a font of informa-tion about storytelling and Readers' Theatre. You're sure to find scripts that would interest your students at his absorbing website. (See *www.aaronshep.com/rt/index/html*)

Teaching Is a Work of Heart (*www.teachingheart.net/ readerstheater.htm*)

This site is chock-a-block with scripts and other useful links related to outstanding children's literature by authors such as Isaac Bashevis

Singer and Madeleine L'Engle. Young readers will appreciate the script titled "This Is Your Life, Amelia Bedelia!" Also, be sure to see the multicultural folktales. (See *www.geocities.com/EnchantedForest/Tower/3235/index.html*)

ESSENTIAL LITERACY PRACTICE 3: COMPREHENSION

How can you deepen students' understanding of what they read? How can you use electronic tools to help students analyze and interpret the written word when reading both traditional and multimedia texts?

Every reader, if he has a strong mind, reads himself into the book, and amalgamates his thoughts with those of the author.
—Johann Wolfgang von Geothe

Ultimately reading comes down to being able to construct meaning from texts and graphics. Proficient readers excel at deriving meaning from an assortment of texts. They can engage with text and graphics on an intellectual and often emotional level. Less skilled readers, on the other hand, seldom become invested in what they're reading, except perhaps when they're passionate about the subject. All too often less skilled readers are eager for the reading period to be over so they can get on with activities that they find more dynamic.

Why Do Many Students Have Difficulty Understanding and Interpreting What They Read?

Often a lack of *schema*, or background information, is a particular problem for less skilled readers. For example, what are their chances of understanding a chapter about the Civil War in a social studies textbook if they lack background knowledge about this period in history? This problem can be especially acute for English Language Learners (ELLs). Children from other countries must learn to cope with a new language and culture as well as come to terms with textbooks that require immense amounts of background knowledge.

In addition, specialized vocabulary words can be challenging for students with limited word knowledge. It stands to reason that youngsters who are unfamiliar with the word *emancipation* will struggle with a passage that discusses the freeing of slaves during the Civil War era. An essential building block for making meaning would be missing. Further, textbooks are often written in a way that make accessing information difficult. Much is taken for granted about the reader's understanding of the world and cultural literacy.

Sometimes the problem is not with the text itself. Many students are willing to let the text wash over them. If an assigned reading has little relevance to their lives, they decide to coast. (For insights into this phenomenon see the book *Reading Don't Fix No Chevy's: Literacy in the Lives of Young Men,* by Michael W. Smith and Jeffrey D. Wilhelm, Heinemann, 2002.)

While new media can't solve all these problems, they can be brought to bear on students' ability to comprehend texts. In this section I discuss two synergistic processes: building schema, or building blocks for understanding and deepening students' ability to respond to and interpret what they read.

What Do Experts Recommend?

The more engaged we are with what we're reading, the more likely we are to understand and interpret what we have read. Our response to a text is often highly individualistic and personal. That is, we interpret texts differently from each other, and even from the way we might have interpreted them ourselves at a different point in our lives, theorizes

literary critic Louise Rosenblatt. "Different transactions between readers and texts at different times under different circumstances and for different purposes may produce different interpretations, different 'works,'" posits Rosenblatt.[23] Rosenblatt's theory, called "Reader Response," dates from 1938, and is still well respected. One of Rosenblatt's fundamental ideas is that the text itself isn't the authority; it's the *interaction* between reader and text that is essential. *Meaning resides somewhere between the two.*

What are the implications of the Reader Response theory for practice? Once we've asked students to interact with text, how can we help them connect with what they're reading and interpret ideas? And what happens when we add new media to the equation?

A New Text Genre Helps Students Engage with Text

"What is the use of a book," thought Alice in Wonderland, "without pictures or conversation?" Clearly Alice was ahead of her time. Multimedia texts that contain elements such as sounds, images, film clips, and online glossaries can enhance comprehension. For example, an adolescent who "views" a multimedia text of *Romeo and Juliet* may experience the text quite differently from a classmate who reads the original, unembellished script. Media experts Bruner and Tally call works that have been augmented with music, hyperlinks, video clips, and photos "expanded books." They explain that "an expanded book puts a central work of print, film, or video into a wider context. . . In the case of a book, the additional material and context might include interactive illustrations and clips of the author introducing the book or scholars responding to it." Thus, these digital hybrids amplify the context in which students learn.[24] The addition of media can also boost students' level of engagement when they read specifically to develop schema.

Implications of Hypertext for Teaching

Can hypertext capabilities help students comprehend what they read? Yes. With hypertext, different types of students can read texts for different purposes. In contrast to the monolithic, linear texts of old, hypertexts allow students to read different "branches" or segments of texts for different purposes. They can use electronic texts to explore a topic by *category*, such as geography or biography. Hypertext also allows readers to cross-reference a subject using an online reference tool such as *Encarta Encyclopedia Deluxe* (Microsoft) or *Grolier Multimedia Encyclopedia*. These tools encourage critical thinking; they allow students to analyze subjects from various perspectives.

Surprisingly this nonlinear approach to making meaning is not new. The ability to move back among texts was presaged by scholars who studied Aristotle's notes and lectures by moving back and forth among fragments of original texts to construct a coherent whole. To this day scholars use this method for their research. But today this sort of detective work—rereading and back-and-forthing—has become much easier through the use of digital texts, which have changed the nature of students' relationship with reference materials.[25]

For another example of how a different type of expanded text can aid students' comprehension, consider Chaucer's *Canterbury Tales*. The combination of Middle English and obscure words, combined with a lack of background knowledge, has bewildered many an English major. But today's scholars can take advantage of websites devoted to Chaucer. They can read original texts, hear words pronounced, and discover their meanings. They can learn about Chaucer's life and the world he inhabited. Beyond that, scholars can compare interpretations, literary criticism, and so on, without needing to track down a dozen library books. Hypertext makes classic works vastly more accessible.

Try It!

You may develop a whole new take on Geoffrey Chaucer now that his work is more accessible.

- Chaucer, G. *Canterbury Tales*, available online at the University of Virginia. (See *etext.virginia.edu/mideng.browse.html*)
- Undergraduate websites:
  icg.fas.harvard.edu/~chaucer/pronunciation
  icg.fas.harvard.edu/~enge115b
  www.unc.edu/depts/chaucer (Here you'll find Chaucer meta-page with links to an audio recording of *Canterbury Tales*.)[26]

Similarly, if Shakespeare is part of your curriculum, you can become a member of the new Globe Theatre in London. For example, Amy Wenig, a teacher of high school honors English in Berlin, Wisconsin, engaged her students in conversation with members of the Globe Theatre Company, 4,000 miles away. She set up a live video chat. Students were able to talk with actors about different Shakespearean roles, whether tradition dictated that boys and men played all the roles, and so on. Diane Curtis of the George Lucas Educational Foundation (GLEF) reports that, "Typically youngsters who might have balked at what they thought was impenetrable language are hooked, partly because Shakespeare deals 'with big, elemental subjects—power, love, death," Hurley [an actor at the Globe Theatre] remarks that students become absorbed in Shakespeare's works because "he addresses them as a human being, not as a politician. He's a poet, a philosopher."[27]

The New Globe Theatre, Dedicated to Educating the World About Shakespeare

Although live video conferences with the Globe Theatre actors are pricey ($240 for an hour session), becoming a member of Globelink is only $50 a year *per school*. Globelink offers a wealth of audio and text resources including notes on costume and set design and an interview with a director. See *www.shakespearesglobe.org/navigation/framesetNS.htm*[28]

Fiction Meets Hypertext

While we've all used hypertext to research nonfiction topics, a lesser known application involves fiction. That is, some literary critics argue that hypertext is changing the way we read and understand fiction. They also wonder whether hypertext fiction represent completely new genre? Although still considered the province of the avant-garde, hypertext fiction has been around for a few decades. Rather than being available online, hypertext books were originally published the traditional way. You may have seen the "Choose Your Own Adventure" series, which allows readers to travel different paths by offering choices at the end of a chapter. For instance, in "Secret of the Ninja," by Jan

Leibold, the premise involves you, the reader, who has traveled to Japan to master an ancient martial art. But a friend, Nada, hands you a mystery to solve about a terrible curse that's been haunting her. To save Nada and yourself, you must solve a mystery. How you go about it depends on the choices you make, as in *"If you decide to go back for the mirror, turn to page 41; If you decide to keep climbing, turn to page 48."*[29] Several of the children I've taught were big fans of this series; they liked the sense of controlling the plot. In fact, students usually wanted to reread the adventures to see how different choices affected the ending. My students must not have been the only fans— in 1998 there were over 250 of these "choose your own adventure" books in print.[30]

While interactive books may not appeal to everyone, students who do become captivated by them benefit in many ways. They interact with texts in ways that can result in dramatic increases in comprehension. Middle school language arts teacher Pat Harder, for example, has her students create their own "Create Your Own Adventure" stories using media to help them create different plot lines. Students begin by using Inspiration software to create conceptual maps of the stories they want to tell, often based on their lives. Then they add to their maps using contrasting shapes and lines that show the progression of their ideas. Ms. Harder observes,

> For the kids, it's the first time we look at information architecture, and we talk about how simple it is to change the color and shape of certain bubbles or nodes and symbols so that at each level of information, there is a color and a shape—that by looking at it immediately, the kids start to see, 'Oh, these types of information are analogs to one another.'[31]

Enticing the "Net Generation" Reader

Many children's books take a nonlinear approach to telling a story. In fact, the nature of children's books began to shift with the advent of television. Once we had this extraordinary device in our homes, with its "instant connectivity," we took the first steps toward becoming a global village.[32] The early pioneers who played with form in children's literature include Maurice Sendak, John Burningham, Anthony Browne, and Chris Van Allsburg. These authors addressed children as intelligent, sophisticated readers. Their books encompass themes such as death, hardships, and life's ironies. Although at first some resisted these books, they eventually gained a wide readership. Thus, with books that were often more gritty than sweet, these authors had set the stage for further experimentation. Today these avant-garde works sit on the same shelf as more traditional styles of children's literature.[33]

Although many readers prefer to have the author cast a spell over them, in the form of a powerful narrative, that doesn't rule out traditional literary devices such as flashbacks, foreshadowing, and such. The point is that today both authors and readers can choose how they wish to interact with texts.

Online Resources for Developing Comprehension and Engagement with Texts

Digital books abound on the Web. One classic example is Project Gutenberg, a site that offers 6,200 free texts. You can download them and print them out, import them into an electronic book, or read them on your computer screen. Another great resource, notable for its multicultural offerings, is "The International Children's Digital Library," for students from three through twelve years old. At present the site offers 200 titles from 27 countries. Fifteen languages are represented. Unfortunately, as of this writing the site is a little hard to use, but the potential benefits are enormous.[34]

Where to Find All Sorts of Digital Texts

Project Gutenberg

The first of its kind (established in 1971), this resource makes eBooks or eTexts available to everyone all over the world. Come here to find everything from Shakespeare's plays to Sherlock Holmes mysteries. (See *Promo.net/pg* and consider volunteering or making a donation.)

Alex: A Catalog of Electronic Texts on the Internet

Another exceptional resource, The Alex Catalogue, also invites visitors to download public domain texts free. You can search by title, author, or date. (See *www.infomotions.com/alex/*)

The International Children's Digital Library

A gold mine of children's picture books from all over the world. Ultimately, the developers of this site hope to offer approximately 10,000 books, representing 100 cultures, to everyone. (See *www.icdlbooks.org/*)

Aesop's Fables: Online Collection

Great for students of all ages, this site offers more that 625 fables, some of which are available in audio format. Be sure to see these bonuses: background information on Aesop's life and 120 fairy tales by Hans Christian Anderson. (See *www.aesopfables.com*)

Developing Curricular Units

- Score CyberGuides

You and your students can use CyberGuides, which are supplementary, standards-based, instructional "packages." Each guide focuses on a work of literature. Packages include a student and teacher edition, standards, a task and a process by which it may be completed, teacher-selected websites, and a rubric based on California Language Arts Content Standards. (See *www.sdcoe.k12.ca.us/SCORE/cyberguide.html*)

Adolescents Publish in E-'zines

If you teach adolescents, you may want to invite them to submit their essays and fictional pieces to electronic magazines. Called e-zines, these venues can provide middle-grade students with a mature forum for self-expression. Merlyn's Pen is one of the best. (See *www.merlynspen.com*, or contact via snail mail at P.O. Box 910, East Greenwich, RI 02828.)

ESSENTIAL LITERACY PRACTICE 4: VOCABULARY

Vocabulary development and comprehension are two sides of the same coin. How can you help students use digital media to help them broaden and deepen their understanding of words and their ability to use them to communicate?

. . . anybody who writes down to children is simply wasting. . . time. You have to write up, not down. Children are demanding. . . Children love words that give them a hard time, provided they are in a context that absorbs their attention.
—E. B. White

Vocabulary knowledge and the ability to comprehend texts go hand in hand. Hundreds of studies bear out this simple truth. Show me a student with a well-developed vocabulary, a student who can not only recite definitions for many words, but who has internalized their nuances and meanings, and I'll show you a student with strong comprehension skills.

Why It's So Hard to Master New Words

Students typically learn from three to twenty new words a day, which can add up to 3,000 to 7,000 new words a year, according to vocabulary experts Beck and McKeown.[35] But how do students learn the meanings of words? Typically word knowledge comes from several encounters with a target word, in different contexts. And if each of these encounters offers rich clues about its meaning, so much the better. For example, a sentence such as "Katrina sat down to put on her *galoshes* because it had rained all morning long and the streets were flooded," is much richer than "Katrina put on her *galoshes*." The first sentence offers many more context clues for understanding *galoshes* than the second. But you can't always count on texts to offer this level of support.

Another problem with learning new words relates to the way glossaries are written. Figuring out a word's meaning by looking it up in a glossary can often prove more bewildering than enlightening. One issue is that the glossary's definition may be circular. Another is that the exemplar sentence may use the target word in a way that's inconsistent with how it's used in the original text. Finally, the words used to explain the target word are often rarely used words themselves, leaving the reader in the dark.

But there are more pressing problems. Some students have a *language-learning disability* that makes it difficult for them to learn new words. This disability affects all facets of language learning from learning sound/symbol associations to understanding word meaning. This is a congenital disorder.[36] In my experience, many students with this disorder benefit from multimodal experiences with words, such as speaking, writing, listening, and creating art to capture word meaning. Taking new word cards home and practicing them with parents and siblings has also proven to be effective.

Many experts in second language acquisition believe that the relationship between vocabulary learning and comprehension is a prime topic for further study. But we do know that English Language Learners face special hurdles in vocabulary development, and therefore need even more practice using both implicit and explicit instructional strategies.[37] One such challenge is that despite the fact that many ELLs are enthusiastic about learning new words, they often find it particularly challenging to *apply* them to novel contexts. This disconnect between instruction and actual reading makes it difficult for ELLs to keep up with native English speakers who are mastering thousands of new words a year.[38]

HOW DO YOU KNOW WHEN A STUDENT KNOWS A WORD?

What does it mean to *know* a word? To have truly mastered a word, a child needs to have encountered it many times, in a variety of contexts. Steven Stahl's research revealed that vocabulary development is a dynamic process. That is, word knowledge can be best understood as a continuum characterized by the following three stages, in order of increasing sophistication.[39]

- *Association processing:* a child can use a synonym for the new word or explain how it relates to what's being read.
- *Comprehension processing:* a child demonstrates an understanding of a new word through activities such as matching, filling in the blank, etc., which require mastery beyond rote learning.
- *Generation processing:* a child knows how to use the new word in an altogether new context. Children who have reached this advanced stage can retrieve a word spontaneously.

Getting to the generative processing stage with many words is definitely the goal. To do so, students need see the word used in rich and varied ways, especially if they're learning words that don't simply represent shades of meaning for words they already know (such as *frigid* for *cold*), but involve sophisticated understandings (such as *pilgrim, democracy,* or *photosynthesis*).

How many words should we expect children to learn? Experts have been debating this question for eons. It's hard to pin down a number because of the great variability introduced by socioeconomic factors and teaching styles. But current estimates suggest that students in grades three through nine typically learn 3,000–4,000 words per school year.[40]

How do students acquire word knowledge? There are two schools of thought. One is that *incidental word learning* is the most effective method. To learn words incidentally, children need to read often; broad exposure to words both enlarges their vocabulary and helps them understand relationships among words. According to this method, to really understanding a word is a result of encountering it *many* times in a natural context. The other school of thought maintains that incidental word learning is too scattershot to be effective; a more systematic approach, with *direct instruction,* is best. But, many argue, there is often not enough time in the school day to provide the amount of direct instruction that's called for. For example, if a teacher assigns a list of twenty-five vocabulary words per week for intensive study, she will only "cover" 900 words in a thirty-six-week school year.

Reading experts Jeanne Chall and Catherine Snow point out that these two approaches are not mutually exclusive.[41] Many teachers achieve impressive results by combining the two methods. This makes infinite sense to me! In so doing, we need to bear in mind two points: First, not surprisingly, research demonstrates that children who spend the most time engaged in *recreational reading* have the most robust vocabularies.[42] Second, when we offer students *explicit instruction that includes Latin and Greek roots,* we give them tools to unlock the meanings of scores of other words, particularly in content areas in the upper grades. This is because 60 percent of the words in the English language derive from Latin and Greek roots. If, for instance, a child knows that *bio-* refers "life" and *-ology* means "the study of," she can understand *biology.* By extension, she can understand *geology, zoology,* and so on. Thus, the generative method offers a big return on a relatively small investment of time. In fact, teaching students how to combine the most useful roots (such as *bene-* and *bon-*, which mean *good*, as in *beneficial* and *bonus*) with just twenty of the most common prefixes (such as *a-* or *an-* which means *without* or *not*, as in *amoral, amorphous,* and *atypical*) and suffixes (*-graph*, an instrument for writing, as in *telegraph*) helps them understand about *100,000 new words!*[43]

Two Excellent Books for Vocabulary Instruction

These two books offer classroom-based ideas for making word study an integral part of classroom life. The authors also promote fun, using techniques such as word walls, the study of opposites, and practice of math terminology using trade books such as *Math Curse* by Jon Scieszka and Lane Smith and *Anno's Mysterious Multiplying Jar* by Mitsumasa Anno.

- Camille L. Blanchowicz and P. Fisher, *Teaching Vocabulary in All Classrooms* (Upper Saddle River, NJ: Prentice Hall, 1996).
- Janet Allen, *Words, Words, Words* (York, ME: Stenhouse, 1999).

What Effective Practices Can You Use for Your Vocabulary Instruction?

The box that follows is my synthesis of the research literature on best practices.[44] I recommend spending twenty minutes a day on vocabulary instruction if at all possible. The payoffs will be astounding when vocabulary practice and word play become part of the fabric of classroom life. Mainly, students' ability to comprehend texts will soar!

Six Goals for Research-Based Vocabulary Instruction

1. *Relate the new to the known.* Show the interrelatedness of words and how they fit into students' existing schema.
2. *Promote active, in-depth processing* (as in Stahl's three-stage continuum, discussed earlier).

3. *Offer multiple exposures of target words.* Read the target word, use it in a context-rich sentence, generate many sentences, and display them in the classroom.

4. *Help students become strategic readers.* Two suggestions are 1) Teach students how to use context clues to unlock meaning; and 2) Show them how to use structural analysis to make sense of unfamiliar words. For example, show how to figure out the meaning of *poisonous* by combining knowledge of the word *poison* with *-ous,* which in this instance means "full of."

5. *Have students increase the volume of their reading.* William Nagy and Patricia Herman estimate that a child who reads 25 minutes a day for 200 days will increase his or her vocabulary by 750 to 1,500 words a year. Not bad, when you take the long view.[45]

6. *Create a climate in which everyone enjoys words and word play.* Engage students in word puzzles, crosswords, rhyming patterns, and opportunities to share words that enlighten, amuse, or amaze. Display the collection in a prominent place and add to it daily or weekly.

How Can Technology Help Foster Vocabulary Development?

Computers alone cannot foster true vocabulary learning; teachers are much more effective when it comes to mediating children's encounters with unfamiliar words. But new media *can* act as a catalyst for students' vocabulary development in a number of important ways. Informational CD-ROMs, for example, can help build students' *schema,* or cognitive structures related to abstract subjects and events. Given that vocabulary learning requires multiple exposures to words, new tools can help by offering novel experiences with specialized vocabulary (for example, in all words related to snakes or volcanoes).

Websites, or traditional practice books, devoted to word families, Latin and Greek roots, and word meanings in many languages, can be enormously helpful for learning about new words and their derivation. Some sites offer games or puzzle makers that make studying words fun.

Software products that encourage students to apply new word knowledge to problem-solving situations or crossword puzzles can entice.

Use the Web to Build Your Students' Vocabulary

WordZap is a game you can play over the Net or against the computer; it's aimed at people who love Scrabble and Boggle. (See *www.wordzap.com/*)

For an online dictionary it's hard to beat **Webster's Online**. Sign up for the free word a day feature that's delivered to your email account. (See *www.m-w.com/netdict.htm*)

Word investigations wouldn't be complete without consulting this great online **thesaurus** offered by the University of Chicago. (See *humanities.uchicago.edu/forms_unrest/ROGET.html*)

At **Word Wizard** children can play with language. They can also define slang terms and add them to "Slang Street," a linked resource. (See *www.wordwizard.com/*)

Did you ever wonder about the origins of unusual words such as persnickety or flabbergast? If so, find out more at **Word Detective.** (See *www.word-detective.com/backidx.html*)

At **Puzzle Maker** students can create their own crossword puzzles to reinforce vocabulary. (See *www.puzzlemaker.School.Discovery.com*)

Just what young children need: A **picture dictionary.** This one is available in several languages including French, Spanish, Portuguese, and German. (See *www.EnchantedLearning.com/dictionary.html*)

For English Language Learners

Wordskills.com offers language resources—for example, "phrasal verb of the day," and games that emphasize skills such as syllable stress—for students, teachers, and trainers. (See *www.wordskills.com*)

Where can older ESL students go for advice on their writing and resources to help them learn idioms, spelling, grammar, in addition to online courses? Here's one idea: **OWL Resources,** developed by Purdue University. (See *owl.english.purdue.edu/handouts/esl/eslstudent.html*)

Word processing software products, with their built-in dictionaries and thesauri, offer insights into word meaning at the "teachable moment"—that is, *while* children are composing or editing their work. Here, for example, is a strategy that teacher Doris Brosnan uses with her third-graders. Weary of worn-out words such as *sad, nice, good,* and *big,* Ms. Brosnan challenges her students to find alternatives by consulting the thesaurus. In the case of the word *sad,* for example, and its multiple synonyms, she models how to decide among *unhappy, depressed, blue, downhearted,* or *dejected* as the best alternative given the nuanced meaning the child seeks.[46] Such explorations of shades of meaning can be reinforced by creating word webs (in this example *sad* would be in the middle of the web, with the synonyms and exemplar sentences radiating outward).

In a different vein, do you have all sorts of reference-oriented CD-ROMs piled up in a technology closet in your school? If so, dust off those digital encyclopedias, atlases, zoo tours, and underwater explorations, and have students study the subjects they're most curious about; they will be expanding their specialized vocabulary knowledge at the same time. Invite students to keep track of new word families by creating a word wall near the classroom computer area.

More Outstanding Resources for Vocabulary Development

A Digital Dictionary

What if students could hold the entire contents of *Merriam Webster's Collegiate Dictionary* in the palm of their hands? With the Franklin dictionary, students can. They can also access words and synonyms, as well as hear each target word pronounced. (See *www.Franklin.com*)

Becoming Word Experts

For students in grades 2–12, try out *Wordly Wise,* a series of books designed to stretch students' lexical knowledge by having them complete activities such as hidden messages and crossword puzzles. For students in grades 7–11 check out "Vocabulary from Classical Roots," a series that demonstrates how to apply Latin and Greek roots when figuring out word meanings. Both series are from Educators Publishing Service. (See *www.epsbooks.com*)

Telecommunications tools offer ways for children to try new words when composing messages to various correspondents (as in keypals) from all over. Children can also write to online experts to seek answers for their questions related to science. A great all-around resource is "Pitsco's Ask an Expert," which offers students the chance to write to hundreds of experts "ranging from astronauts to zookeepers." (See *www.askanexpert.com/*)

Last but not least, if you've given up on television as a learning tool, it's time to take another look. *Reading Rainbow,* which premiered twenty years ago on the Public Broadcasting System (PBS), has been recognized for excellence by literacy organizations such as the International Reading Association and the National Council for Teachers of English, and has won two Emmy awards. Because of the program's emphasis on science, many segments use specialized vocabulary words related to topics such as the rainforest or weather. For example, in a segment entitled "Hail to Mail," a young stamp collector explains the vocabulary words he uses, as in this excerpt:

> This stamp is in *mint condition,* which means that *it's never, ever been used.* And it has *full gum,* which is the *glue on the back of the stamp.* And what we have here are called *perforations. The perforations are what connects the stamps to other stamps when you buy them.* And this stamp has *fine engraved detail,* which means it has *very, very small designs.*[47]

In addition, the program's host, LeVar Burton, frequently engages in word play. In a segment about a duck, Burton remarks that something "isn't all it's *quacked* up to be."[48] (The program is geared for five- to eight-year-olds.) Check the PBS website for local listings (*www.pbs.org*) and your library for the featured books. Also see *gpn.unl.edu/rainbow* for games and activities based on particular episodes.

ESSENTIAL LITERACY PRACTICE 5: READING AND WRITING ACROSS THE CURRICULUM

Accomplished readers are avid readers. They read nonfiction texts on topics as far-ranging as Venus or ancient Greece. How can you encourage students to delve into the topics that interest them? How can you use the Web, CD-ROM–based magazines and encyclopedias, and multimedia reference books to augment their studies? Finally, how can you teach students to use online resources both wisely and ethically?

Children love reading about real things. It gives them an understanding of our world and the way things work. And considering all the newspapers, brochures, guides, maps, Internet sites, and how-to manuals we navigate as adults, it's safe to say that nonfiction is the genre children will read most often when they grow up.
—Sharon Taberski[49]

Why Is Reading Nonfiction Texts So Difficult?

Exposure to nonfiction texts—magazines such as *TIME for Kids*, newspapers, reports, and information books—stimulates children's imaginations and prepares them to describe, explain, and predict natural phenomena. Nonfiction texts also help students understand the natural world and the interconnectedness of all living things. Lack of exposure to nonfiction texts can have a negative impact on a student's school career. Consider this: The average score for students who reported having all four of these types of texts in their home—books, magazines, newspapers, encyclopedias—was higher than those who reported having fewer reading materials, according to "The Nation's Report Card".[50]

Incredible as digital resources are, they can prove a double-edged sword for learners. On one hand they can open new worlds to young researchers. On the other hand, hypertext documents can tempt students to plagiarize, given the ease of cutting and pasting published works into one's own document. And with their branching structures, they can be a boon or a distraction depending on the learner's ability to stay focused on a search without getting derailed by irrelevant information or flashy advertisements. Another concern is that students may access unreliable sources, of which there is no shortage.

Evaluating Information Sources

Teaching students to evaluate Internet information critically

See the professional journal, *Reading On Line*, for useful tips. (See *www.readingonline.org/editorial/edit_index.asp*?HREF=*december2001/index.html*)

Internet Detectives

The result of a collaborative effort across Wisconsin, students have evaluated websites themselves as an alternative to filtering software. (See *www.madison.k12.wi.us/tnl/detectives*)

Teacher Helpers: Critical Evaluation Information

Once again educational technology guru Kathy Schrock comes through with practical guidelines for educators. (See *school.discovery com/schrockguide/eval.html/*)

Evaluating Web Resources

An excellent option for teacher trainers, this web site offers an online module through which participants learn to evaluate resources. PowerPoint slides included for conducting seminars. (See *www2.widener. edu/Wolfgram-Memorial-Library/webevaluation/webeval.htm*)

Beyond that, locating accurate information that's written on the right grade level, with just the right number of challenging vocabulary words for every student in your classroom, is a daunting task. English Language Learners (ELLs) deserve particular consideration; acquiring knowledge in English poses special challenges for students who may be fluent in English socially, but not academically. Bear in mind that it may take an ELL student five to seven years to catch up to native English–speaking peers, according to Language expert, James Cummins.[51] We need to give them all the support we can as they learn vital concepts in content area topics.

Despite these drawbacks, reading content area texts can be richly rewarding for students, even in the primary grades. Information books can motivate them to read and learn. You've probably noticed how much children enjoy just plain *knowing things*. They take delight in applying what they read about to real-world situations—how to cultivate a vegetable garden or how bees make honey. Not only that. Many literacy experts, including Chall, Jacobs, and Baldwin, hypothesize that greater emphasis on informational books in the primary grades can help students avoid the "fourth-grade slump," which is of particular concern with poor children. Briefly, many fourth-graders have difficulty making the transition from stage two of reading development (typically acquired in grades 1 through 3) in which they're "learning to read," to stage three of reading development, in which they're "reading to learn." Stage three, typically acquired in grades 4 through 8, is characterized by the numerous cognitive demands placed upon the reader (see Part 3 for Chall's Stages of Reading Development).[52]

Children who have difficulty making the transition from *learning to read* to *reading to learn* are at a great disadvantage academically. They must compete against students who have read broadly and deeply in nonfiction subject areas—children who have had many opportunities to satisfy their curiosity about the universe. These information-rich children will be way ahead of the game when it comes to their ability to learn from the sorts of nonfiction materials (i.e., textbooks) that will be required reading in the upper-elementary grades. They'll be able to draw upon a deep reservoir of specialized vocabulary words to help them make sense of the world and all that they're learning. How can we level the playing field?

Promoting Real Learning in the Content Areas

First, decide what sort of pedagogical framework you use to guide your content area teaching. Second, ask yourself what your big goals are. Third, think through what concepts you want your students to *really* understand? (None of this is easy, so expect this process to take some time.)

"Nurturing understanding is one of the loftiest aspirations of education and also one of the most elusive," points out Tina Blythe and her associates in their book, *The Teaching for Understanding Guide.* "The very concept of understanding raises a host of complex questions for thoughtful educators," Blythe continues, "What does it mean to understand something?... How do we know how well they [students] understand something?..."[53]

Blythe and her colleagues at Harvard's Project Zero have developed a framework for deepening students' understanding of any curricular topic. Called Teaching for Understanding (TfU), this four-pronged approach to conceptualizing math, science, and social studies units has

T*he* F*our* C*ornerstones of* T*eaching for* U*nderstanding* (TfU)

1. **Choose a *generative* topic, meaning that it is focused around a few main ideas and allows students to make a personal connection.** Once you've established your generative topic, students can engage in genuine inquiry. (*Nongenerative topic*: the distance of planets from the sun. *Generative topic*: the interrelatedness of planets in our solar system and how they were formed.)

2. **Be sure your understanding goals are clear and explicit.** This can mean posting them in the classroom. It can mean daily discussions in which you meet with students to discuss and reflect on their overarching goals.

3. **Have students demonstrate their understanding early and often.** You might have students collaborate, reflect on their own work, or display their work-in-progress. As for your role, variety is the key. You might serve as a coach, lecturer, leader, participant in discussions, and so on.

4. **Consider assessment a part of the fabric of classroom life.** That way you'll know whether your students are getting it or not because you assess them frequently. This doesn't mean formal tests and pop quizzes. Talk to students informally. Be spontaneous. Encourage them to critique each other's work and make revisions. Figure out ways to have students *share* the responsibility for assessing what they've learned.[54]

gained currency with teachers across the country. In the accompanying box is a quick summary of this method.

To my thinking the TfU approach has three clear benefits. First, it's an infinitely flexible approach to most any content subject area. Once a teacher has internalized the process, he can apply it to topics as diverse as fractions or electricity. Second, TfU puts teachers in charge; they're not asked to follow scripts. This approach gives them a chance to call the shots. And third, many teachers comment that TfU empowers their students. Students are viewed as an integral part of teaching and learning, not empty vessels into which we pour facts and figures.[55]

How Can You Use Technology to Support Teaching for Understanding?

At what point would it be advantageous for TfU and technology to converge? Where are some of the potential intersections? As an example of how to use new tools to support the TfU approach, imagine that you are beginning a study of marine life. You might begin by showing a video about ocean life to the entire class so everyone has a common jumping-off point. After establishing generative questions (such as *What characteristics do these ocean creatures share? What physical properties help them adapt to their environment?*), you and your students are ready to create clear and explicit understanding goals (such as *Students will understand marine ecosystems;* and *Students will develop their understanding of environmental issues related to the particular marine life they investigate).* A volunteer captures these goals using a wordprocessing tool, prints them out, and displays them in the classroom.

Once students are clear on the understanding goals, they begin their research on oceanlife, drawing from as many sources as possible—traditional books, the Internet (with bookmarked links to preselected sites), and encyclopedias, both real and virtual (*Encarta*, for example).

Web-based Tool for Developing Curricular Units

Designed primarily for teachers, **TrackStar** helps organize and annotate a collection of websites around a curriculum unit. For example, if you're studying humpback whales and have five key sites you want students to explore, this is the tool for you. TrackStar makes it possible to line up the five sites and annotate them (e.g., Be sure to read about what whales eat). You can also search databases of ready-made tracks, adapt them for your class, and post your own "tracks." (See *trackstar.hprtec.org*)

Students create their final research paper using a variety of new tools. They create a database of marine life found in the Pacific Ocean during the research phase. They write their reports on a word processor, importing diagrams and illustrations into their documents.

Students are required to meet at regular intervals to comment on each others' work in progress. You decide to capture the work they share at these meetings and archive it using an electronic portfolio that will become part of your assessment program.

Electronic Assessment Portfolios

Multiple Intelligences and Portfolios: A Window into the Learner's Mind by Evangeline Harris-Stefanakis (Heinemann)
This book provides a lively discussion of how culture, environment, and language all play into a student's intelligence. The accompanying CD-ROM offers actual examples of student work and how it developed over time.

"Beck's Bits and Bytes"
Technology specialist, Sandy Beck of Cummin, Georgia, discusses the advantages of online portfolios and how to create them. (See *www.forsyth.k12.ga.us/sbeck/writing/*)

For a more formal assessment, you work with students to devise an *electronic* rubric to capture the desired characteristics of a project. This process can jump-start a conversation in which students compare the characteristics of a *good* research report with those of an *outstanding* research report.

Primary Source Material to Enhance Social Studies Units

Primary source material that at one time could be accessed only by visiting museums is now just a few clicks away. For example, you can access Civil War photographs, letters written by Abraham Lincoln, the Civil Rights movement, and Jefferson's handwritten draft of the Declaration of Independence, to name but a few treasures. Check out these sources:

■ "WayBack: U.S. History for Kids." (See *www.pbs.org/wgbh/amex/kids*)
■ Library of Congress. (See *memory.loc.gov/*)[56]

These are just a few ideas for research projects. You can devise a completely different scenario based on *your* curriculum, students, and the media you're able to get your hands on.

Handheld Computers and Detachable Keyboards

When it comes to capturing students' ideas on the fly, consider implementing a writing program that takes advantage of handheld computers and detachable keyboards. At roughly $300 for a small computer (detachable keyboard included), many teachers are able to outfit their students with this combination of portable tools without paying a king's ransom. For example, fifth-grade teacher Tony Vincent in Omaha, Nebraska, has been using them since the 2001–2002 school year. He believes these tiny computers, which, ironically, are more powerful than the PCs of the 1980s, have had a strong impact on his students' writing abilities in all subject areas. As reporter Roberta Furger notes:

> Students use the small devices to record, graph, and chart observations and to animate cell structures in science. In math, they use a variety of free software to create and solve word and numeric problems. They use handhelds to surf the Web, manage classroom projects, and share their work with peers.[57]

These small devices also make passing documents back and forth for peer review very easy. Students can easily send comments on articles or essays back and forth, fostering collaboration. (For more information about Vincent's experiences with handhelds see *www.mpsomoha.org/willow/p5.*)

ESSENTIAL LITERACY PRACTICE 6: WRITING

Word processors are a natural ally for students at all stages of the writing process. How can students use them in ways that resonate with what it means to be a writer?

Battle-hardened professionals do not see a first draft as a final draft. They expect the first draft to be like a blob of clay that a skilled potter flings onto a

whirling potter's wheel. Potential beauty resides in the blob; it can be brought out by the skilled and delicate touch of the potter's hand.
—Richard Marius [58]

"The Nation's Report Card" Findings: Well-Trained Teachers Make a Substantial Difference

Students in the United States have made modest gains in writing, according to findings of the 2002 National Assessment of Educational Progress (NAEP). Known to many as "The Nation's Report Card," NAEP had *not* traditionally offered writing assessments. The first writing assessment was in 1998; grades 4, 8, and 12 participated. Students were asked to write in particular genres, and were given age-appropriate assignments. For example, fourth-graders were asked to write a persuasive letter to their librarian asking him or her to replace a favorite book that had been stolen. Despite small improvements in scores in some areas, it's clear that we have work to do to close the achievement gap (i.e., gender, with girls outscoring boys; race; and socioeconomic status). Research also underscores the importance of parent involvement. In addition, well-trained teachers can make all the difference in helping all students develop as writers regardless of the socioeconomic level of the community.[59]

To become better writers, students need to have great instruction. They also need to have a real purpose for expressing their ideas, and an authentic audience to respond to their compositions. But this is more easily said than done.

Too Many Kids Are Really Good at Avoiding Writing

Many students find it so difficult to express their ideas in writing that they become experts in *not* writing. These same students may have quick and lively imaginations, a keen interest in the world, and are known as raconteurs among their friends and families. But when confronted by paper and pencil, their desire to communicate evaporates. You've seen this happen, I'm sure. These students become clock watchers or pencil-sharpening experts as soon as you ask them to write their ideas.

Recent research shows that all students need more writing practice, not just those who avoid it. A study called "The Neglected 'R,': The

Need for a Writing Revolution," produced by the National Commission on Writing in America's Schools and Colleges, is a call to arms. The authors of the report argue that writing has not received the recognition it deserves as a cornerstone of learning. Consider these findings from the study:

- Most fourth-grade students spend less than three hours a week writing, which is approximately 15 percent of the time they spend watching television.
- Nearly 66 percent of high school seniors do not write a three-page paper as often as once a month for their English teachers.
- Seventy-five percent of seniors may never receive a writing assignment in history or social studies.
- The senior research project has become an educational curiosity, something rarely assigned because teachers do not have time to correct such projects.[60]

Recommended Practices: Process Writing

Most professional writers do not, in Marius' words, view the first draft as a final draft. Writers create outlines, and then rough drafts. They solicit feedback from peers. They edit. They polish. They expect that it will take a lot of time and several drafts before their piece is ready for publication. Professional writers enact the *process writing* approach that has gained currency in schools throughout the nation during the past few decades.

Briefly, the stages of process writing are: creating a literary climate that supports the writers' workshop approach; brainstorming a topic and prewriting; composing a draft; sharing and peer editing; establishing an individual voice; revising; and publishing.

Many experts have written eloquently about teachers, children, and the writing process. I have been particularly influenced by the books listed in the box that follows, which offer glimpses into several approaches to writers' workshops.

How Can You Use New Tools to Help with Process Writing?

Although most teachers I've talked to use word processors for their own writing—letters, reports, classroom newsletters—when I ask them

> ### Four Books on Writing to Inspire You
>
> - *The Art of Teaching Writing* (new edition), Lucy McCormick Calkins (Heinemann, 1994).
> - *Writing: Teachers and Children at Work*, by Donald Graves (Heinemann, 1983).
> - *A Fresh Look at Writing*, by Donald Graves (Heinemann, 1994).
> - *In the Middle*, by Nancie Atwell (Heinemann, 1999).
>
> In addition, *Sharing and Responding*, by Peter Elbow and Pat Belanoff (Boston: McGraw Hill, 2000) is an excellent resource for adult learners. I've used it with my graduate students to help them respond to each others' drafts in creative and insightful ways.

how their students use computers for writing, the great majority reply that their students use computers only to type the *final drafts* of their compositions. This response always comes as a surprise, because what computers help us do best is compose our ideas and rearrange them in a logical sequence through the easy manipulation of text. As Edward B. Fiske observed over a decade ago,

> Computers are the most important new technology for writing instruction since the invention of the pencil—maybe even more so. Learning to write is essentially self-editing. The craft requires writing and rewriting. For little children, the biggest obstacle to learning to write is the physical act of moving the pencil across the paper, but computers make this unnecessary.[61]

Writing with computers can be a transformative act. Students' work becomes fluid. When they print out what they've written, their writing *looks* good, making it easier to read their work aloud. I've seen even the most unmotivated writers jump at the chance to use EasyBook Deluxe or the Amazing Writing Machine word processing/creativity software.[62]

Digital tools provide students with individual needs with more options for learning, and new tools appear on the scene all the time.

For example, a student who lacks keyboarding skills can learn to type by using software products that blend practice with humorous games. Adaptive "filters" can help students conduct research by transforming any Web page into an interactive space (e.g., by reading aloud the text to students and providing a space for them to take notes online). Students who have difficulty composing can use software products that support them by reading text back to writers, anticipating the next word in a phrase, and generating text from dictation.

The Internet also offers support for authors who need tools, such as a dictionary (in English or other languages), thesaurus, or encyclopedia. For a truly comprehensive analysis, check out L. D. Online, one of the best resources for accommodating students with individual needs (see *ldonline.org*).

Be on the lookout for new products that can support writers at every turn, making it possible for them to be active participants in Writers' Workshops. Share your ideas with your colleagues.

As noted previously, photo journals can be a catalyst for writing. Send students off with as many cameras as you can gather. Have them document their world, or create graphics for a work of fiction. While digital cameras make importing photos into text a snap, you can have 35-mm film developed as a disk or CD-ROM for easy manipulation.

A Case in Point: "Techno Books" Created by First-graders

Cindy Morden's class at Roosevelt Elementary School in Keego Harbor, Michigan, learned how to write, design, produce, and publish what they call "Techno Books." Read about this award-winning project that Morden designed based on the equipment available to her at her school combined with a digital camera, scanner, and Zip™ drive she purchased through grant funds. The project developed as the year evolved, culminating in a PowerPoint book that was recorded on videotape, and narrated by students. Finished books were sent home to share with families. (See *www.westbloomfield.k12.mi.us/roosevelt/second01/morden/techbok.html*)[63]

How Software Can Support Process Writing, Especially for Students with Individual Needs

Task	Tool	How It Helps	Further Information
Keyboarding	Intellikeys	Makes it easier for students to control the keyboard	Intellitools *www.intellitools.com*
	Easy Keys		Rockwell Software *www.rockwell.software.com*
Brainstorming	Inspiration	Makes it easy to create graphic organizers; offers sample diagrams	Inspiration *www.inspiration.com*
	KidPix Deluxe 3	Both help students create digital art as an entry point for writing	The Learning Company *www.learningcompany.com*
	Krazy Art Room		Guru Force *www.guruforce.com*
Composing and Editing	Write: Outloud	Talking word processor; offers students a multisensory approach to writing; also has a talking spell checker	Don Johnston *www.donjohnston.com*
	Intellitalk II	Speaks letters, words, sentences while student types; auditory spell checker; predesigned tools and templates	Intellitools *www.intellitools.com*
	EZ Keys	Designed for physically challenged students, this product simplifies control of the keyboard using a mouse simulation and other features	Words Plus *www.wordsplus.com*
	Co-Writer	Tries to anticipate the next word in a composition; child can select word by clicking	Don Johnston *www.donjohnston.com*

	Dragon Dictate	Allows students to bypass the keyboard altogether; they can control any Windows application using their own voice	NanoPac *www.nanopac.com/ragondictate.htm*
	Ace Publisher	Provides interactive help with spelling and grammar	Mind Play *www.mindplay.com*
	FreeWrite	This is a word processor and spell checker for handhelds	Free through *GoKnow.com*
	Noah Lite	Here's an English language dictionary for handhelds (contains 122,000 words)	Free through *www.arslexis.com/*
Conducting Research	eReader	A "talking browser" that helps children with reading and sight disabilities; adds extra toolbar to the top of the computer screen that can be adapted for any digital text, including Web pages	Center for Applied Special Technologies *www.CAST.org*
	Ask Jeeves for Kids, Infoplease, and BigChalk's Homework Central	Websites to help students zero-in on research questions	*www.ajk.com* *www.infoplease.com/* *www.bigchalk.com1*
Publishing Tools	EasyBook Deluxe Ultimate Writing and Creativity Center	Art and text tools that simplify book making Provides many options for creating and illustrating student stories using pictures, words, sounds, etc.	*www.sunburst.com* *www.learningcompanyschool.com*

How Software Can Support Process Writing, Especially for Students with Individual Needs (*Continued*)

TASK	TOOL	HOW IT HELPS	FURTHER INFORMATION
	PowerPoint and HyperStudio	Supports organizational process in creating presentations	Microsoft *Microsoft.com* Sunburst *www.sunburst.com*
	Timeliner	Offers a structure for creating timelines from scratch or adding to existing ones	Tom Snyder Productions *www.tsp.com*
	PiCoMap	Use for concept mapping or for making connections among vocabulary words on handheld devices	*goknow.com/Products/PiCoMap/*
Publishing on the Web	Young Writers and Candlelight Stories	Children can publish their original works on the Web to share with others.	*www.mystworld.com/youngworld* *www.yam.regulus.com*
	Young Author's Magazine Program	E-'zines offer particularly enticing options for older students	*www.candlelightstories.com*

Global Projects

Do you want your students to communicate with keypals from all over the world? Do you want them to write and receive messages in languages other than English (using a built-in translator, if needed)? ePals, the largest online classroom community, may be the site for you. Your students can also opt to collaborate on creative writing projects in both fiction and nonfiction genres. (See *www.epals.com*)

I hope these ideas for integrating new technologies into your reading and language arts curricula will stimulate your thinking about your teaching. Taken as a whole, all seven essential skills and their potential for enhancement using new tools can be a bit overwhelming. If you're feeling strapped for time, take a moment to close your eyes and ask yourself these questions: *What would my ideal teaching situation look like if I were to integrate (even more) digital media to support readers and writers? Which of my teaching objectives could be addressed more effectively by integrating these tools? What sorts of projects would my students be engaged in? What would I be doing? What would my classroom* look *like? What would it* sound *like?* Once you have established your own unique vision, you'll be well on your way to integrating new tools in ways that will make an important difference for your students.

In Part 3, I'll present one example of how a particular group of students' writing was enhanced by using word processing software and telecommunications tools. You'll see how my own vision took shape and how, with help from talented students and colleagues, it became a reality.

After that, I will turn the spotlight on *you, your* students, and *your* colleagues . . .

In Part 3 of this book, I will take you further into the topic of reluctant writers and how new technologies, particularly telecommunications tools, can help them overcome their aversion to writing by publishing their work for an international audience.

Next, Essential Literacy Practice 7 focuses on instilling a love for reading both in school and during their free time. As G. Wallace Woodworth remarked, "We gathered sticke and kindled a fire, and left it burning. To kindle a fire and leave it burning—that is the aim of all great teachers."

ESSENTIAL LITERACY PRACTICE 7: MOTIVATING RELUCTANT READERS AND WRITERS

Genuine interest in a subject can transform your passive, reluctant readers and writers into active members of a literate community. How can you cultivate the interests of your students? How can you use digital media and educational television to entice them to read more?

> *The habit of reading is the only one I know in which there is no alloy.*
> *It lasts when all other pleasures fade. It will be there to support you*
> *when all other resources are gone. It will be present to you when the energies*
> *of your body have fallen away from you. It will make your hours pleasant to you*
> *as long as you live.*
> —Anthony Trollope

The amount of time students spend reading, combined with what they read, has an enormous impact on every aspect of their academic careers. You won't be surprised to learn that studies show that children who immerse themselves in books have higher general reading scores than reluctant readers. This is especially true for students in grades 2 through 5.[64] As Adams explains, "If we want children to learn to read well, we must find a way to induce them to read lots.... And so the circularity of the situation is extremely important: If we want to induce children to read lots, we must teach them to read well."[65]

Captivating Young Minds

When students read broadly and deeply they gain perspective on the world and their place in it. But how best to motivate reluctant readers is a question that has confounded educators since time immemorial. Developing a passion for reading at a young age increases the odds that children will become life-long readers. Some literacy experts, in fact, maintain that children's reading habits are firmly established by the time they reach sixth grade.

How Much Time Do Children Spend Reading?

Very little, on average. Despite a passionate interest in reading when they enter kindergarten, a general malaise sets in as children advance through the grades. Consider these facts, according to the National Reading Report Card.[66]

- Among fourth-graders, 47 percent read something for pleasure every day.
- Among eighth-graders, only 27 percent read for pleasure daily.
- By twelfth grade, only 24.4 percent read anything for pleasure daily.
- Forty percent of fourth-grade students used the library weekly, but the number dropped to 10 percent by senior year.[67]

How can you capture students' interest early, and hold it through adolescence? Fortunately you have many resources to draw upon, and the number of options increases every day.

Reading Aloud to Children: It Works

Although many of the students enrolled in the Jeanne Chall Reading Lab (which I discuss in detail in Part 3) were fearful of reading aloud, *they loved being read to.* This is hardly surprising. Children wanted to read the same books as their classmates, but difficulties related to decoding, fluency, vocabulary development, and so on, made the books written on their developmental levels too challenging for them to read independently.

The benefits of reading aloud to children are impressive. First, children who have listened to read-alouds often become better independent reader. Over time they come to perceive reading as a gratifying activity. Not only do they develop their vocabularies through listening to literature and nonfiction texts read aloud, they also learn about plot structure in fiction and the way information is organized. Through listening, students' vocabularies increase, and they learn about plot structure and how to organize information. And not surprisingly students who are read to often become better writers.

Two Excellent Read Aloud Guides

- An outstanding guide for developing a read-aloud routine for children is *The Read-Aloud Handbook*, fifth edition, by Jim Trelease (Penguin Books, 2001). A parent and former school volunteer, Trelease makes the practice of reading aloud every day compelling for adults and children. See also *Read All About It!*, which offers more advanced titles for upper-elementary and middle school students.
- *How to Get Your Child to Love Reading*, by Esmé Raji Codell (Algonquin

Books, 2003) offers a wealth of creative ideas to get reading into students' bloodstream, encompassing a variety of age levels and student interests.

Creating a Literary Climate

Does your school offer a literary climate in which reading and writing can flourish? Is it characterized by classroom libraries stocked with interesting fiction and nonfiction books and magazines? Are the walls covered with students' writing and other creations? Do children read and write with a real purpose in mind? Do they share their work with audiences ranging from the school principal, to parents, and even the local historical society?

A Passion for Reading

I've been lucky enough to have witnessed the wildly imaginative lengths teachers will go to when it comes to enticing students to read. Some have initiated a silent reading program. Some have orchestrated radio programs that feature book reviews written and delivered by students. Still others have had great success with reading-buddy programs through which older students read books to children in lower grades. In addition, book fairs and all-out read-out weekends in which students and parents camp out at school and read, have proliferated across the United States. So have literature circles, which involve children meeting in small groups to talk about many predetermined aspects of books (e.g., fanciful words).

There's no one sure-fire way to get kids reading. The goal is to find ways to get kids reading—*often*. In the words of Nelson Mandela, former President of the Republic of South Africa, "A reading nation is a winning nation!"

Setting Up Literature Circles

Literature Circles: Voice and Choice in Book Clubs and Reading Groups, by Harvey Daniels (Stenhouse Publisher, 2002). After describing the benefits of literature circles, Daniels explains in detail how to create them from A to Z.

Tune In!

Listen to a discussion of Online Literature Circles in which I meet with children's author Jon Scieszka and technology specialist Sandy Beck, in a live Web cast. We discuss the advantages of going online with literature circles and how to get started. (See *teacher.scholastic. com/professional/techexpert/forum.asp*)

Additional Resources

Children's Literature Guides.

- Children's Literature Web Guide

One of the best, this extensive website was developed in Australia by Professor David K. Brown at the University of Calgary. It's everything a reading/language arts teacher might hope for, from implementing Readers' Theatre in your classroom to links to journals and book reviews. (See *www.acs.ucalgary.ca/~dkbrown/*)

- Planet Esmé

Created by Esmé Raji Codell, the author of *How to Get Your Child to Love Reading*, this website is like a candy store for those who love children's literature. (See *planetesme.com*)

- Center for the Study of Books in Spanish for Children and Adolescents

This encyclopedic website, developed by a children's librarian at California State University, San Marcos, California, includes book reviews and suggestions for books that are available in both English and Spanish. (See *coyote.csusm.edu/campus_center/csb/english/*)

- Book Links

This is an authoritative website about children's literature developed by the American Library Association. (See *www.ala.org/BookLinks*)

- School Library Journal's "Best Books of the Year"

Stay on top of the waves of new children's literature selections being published every year by bookmarking this site. Four thousand books are reviewed each year. (See *www.slj.com/articles/articles/articlesindex.asp*)

- Carol Hurst's Children's Literature Site

Dedicated children's librarian and author Carol Hurst has created an easy to-search, highly informative website about children's literature. (See *www.carolhurst.com/inex/html*)

Listening to Books. Listening libraries abound, delighting students as they read the book as it's being read aloud. You can choose from a wealth of titles—some are even narrated by the author. Here is a premier selection:

- Books on Tape

www.booksontape.com

- Listening library

www.randomhouse.com/audio/listeninglibrary

- Weston Woods

1-800-243-5020

Adolescent Writers. Joshua Niamehr created the **News By Teens** website as a forum where teens can speak out and learn about the world. Joshua invites teens to join a chatroom, submit book reviews, write articles (Racism, Fix Our Society, and Super Mario! are three titles, as of this writing) and more. A mix of current events (as in today's feature, "The 1st Amendment and Separation of Church and State"), teen commentary, and popular culture, this innovative site might motivate reluctant adolescent writers to join the conversation. (See *www.newsbyteens.com*)

Online Book Discussion Groups. The Book Rap is a place where students from all over the world can discuss books with each other via email. Maintained by teacher Cherrol McGhee, a teacher from Queensland, Australia, this site invites you to sign up for a prearranged discussion or initiate your own exchange with another classroom that's registered with the site. (See *owl.qut.edu.au/oz-teachernet/projects/book-rap/br.html*)

See also **Book Divas**, sponsored by *Seventeen Magazine* and Electric Artists (a marketing firm). The site has more than 650 steady visitors as of this writing. See *BookDivas.com* for discussions of titles such as *Waiting for Godot*.

For how-to advice on helping adolescents launch their own book club, see *teenreads.com*. This site is part of the Book Report network.

On the Perils of Not Reading the Newspaper. . .

Arthur Sultzberger Jr., the publisher of the *New York Times*, remarks, "You won't get into a good school, you won't know your Picassos from your Matisses, you won't know what's playing on your kid's MP3, you won't know who won the pennant, you won't know the price of tea in China, and you certainly won't be part of the informed citizenry that keeps a democracy strong. Additionally," he remarks tongue-in-cheek, "you'll catch more colds, because all newspapers are specially treated with an anticold medication that the pharmaceutical industry invented but won't release to the public."[68]

Get your Students Hooked on News

The newspaper can bridge literacy skills and all subject areas. Three outstanding sites that offer free online newspapers are **TIME for Kids, Scholastic News for Kids,** and **Yahooligans News.** National and international events of our times are presented to children along with news-related games, puzzles, and comprehension questions. Many articles are accompanied by curriculum guides, lesson plans, and relevant links for teachers. (See *www. timeforkids,com/TEK/, teacher.scholastic.com/scholasticnews/,* and *www.yahooligans.com/ content/news*)

ENDNOTES

1. Jeanne S. Chall and Helen M. Popp. *Teaching and Assessing Phonics* (Cambridge, MA: Educators Publishing Service, 1996), 29–30.
2. Marilyn Jager Adams, *Beginning to Read: Thinking and Learning About Print* (Boston: MIT Press, 1990), 31.
3. Paul Cuadros, Greg Land, Sean Scully, and Sora Song, "The New Science of Dyslexia," *Time Magazine,* July 28, 2003, 56.
4. Sally Shaywitz, *Overcoming Dyslexia* (New York: Knopf, 2003), 140.

5. Sora Song, "Is Your Child Dyslexic?" in *Time Magazine*, July 28, 2003, 54. In creating these guidelines Song drew from *Overcoming Dyslexia*, by Sally Shaywitz, and *Straight Talk About Reading*, by Susan Hall and Louisa Moats.

6. Shaywitz, *op. cit.*, 58.

7. Barbara Means, William R. Peneul, and Christine Padilla. *The Connected School* (San Francisco: Jossey-Bass, 2001), 194.

8. Jeanne S. Chall. *Stages of Reading Development* (New York, NY: McGraw-Hill, 1983).

9. This discussion is based on a section I wrote for the Soliloquy Learning Teachers' Guide for *Reading Assistant* (2002).

10. Shaywitz, *op. cit.*, 270.

11. National Institute for Literacy, National Institute of Child Health and Human Development, U.S. Department of Education (September 2001). *Put Reading First: Kindergarten through Grade 3*, 22.

12. J. E. Hasbrouck and G. Tindall. "Curriculum-based Oral Reading Fluency Norms for Students in Grades 2 through 5." *Teaching Exceptional Children*, 1992, 41–44.

13. Cited in Wiley Blevins, *Building Fluency: Lessons and Strategies for Reading Success*, (New York, NY: Scholastic, 2001), 11.

14. Wiley Blevins, *op. cit.*, 10.

15. Joseph K. Torgesen, Carol A. Rashotte, and Ann W. Alexander "Principles of Fluency Instruction in reading. "For example, a child at the 90th percentile of reading ability may read as many words in two days as a child at the 10th percentile reads in an entire year outside the school setting." In *Dyslexia, Fluency, and the Brain*, Maryanne Wolf (ed.) (Timonium, MD: York Press, 2001), 348.

16. Shaywitz, op. cit., 273–4.

17. Steven A. Stahl, K. Heubach, and B. Cramond. (1997). *Fluency-oriented Reading Instruction*. (Research Report No. 79). Athens, GA: National Reading Research Center. Cited in Steven A. Stahl and Melanie Kuhn (March 2002). "Making It Sound Like Language: Developing Fluency. *The Reading Teacher*, 55, No. 6, 583.

18. S. Stahl, K. Heubach, and B. Cramond, *Fluency-oriented Reading Instruction*, p. 583.

19. I'm grateful to Marilyn Jager Adams, the well-known literacy researcher and chief scientist at Soliloquy Learning, for inviting me

to help develop this product in the spring of 2002. Reading Assistant offers anthologies for students in grades 2 through 6 that include fiction and nonfiction selections, as well as poems.

20. Marilyn Adams, Personal Communication, Winter 2003.

21. Wiley Blevins, *op. cit.*, 43.

22. Esmé Raji Codell, *How to Get Your Child to Love Reading,* (New York, NY: Workman, 2003).

23. Interview with Louise Rosenblatt. In *Language Arts,* November 1999, 163.

24. Cornelia Bruner and William Tally. *The New Media Literacy Handbook* (New York: Doubleday, 1999), 130.

25. Jay David Bolter, *Writing Space* (Mahwah, NJ: Lawrence Erlbaum, 2001), 110.

26. I am grateful to my colleague, Christopher Mulé, for introducing me to the Chaucer websites, which he learned about in his studies in the English Department of Harvard College.

27. Diane Curtis, "Bandwidth and the Bard." *Edutopia,* Fall 2003, 10.

28. Diane Curtis, *op cit.,* 11.

29. Jay Leibold, *The Secret of the Ninja* (New York: Bantam Books, 1987), 33.

30. Eliza T. Dresang, *Radical Change* (New York: H. W. Wilson Company, 1999), 21.

31. Interview between Milton Chen, executive director of the George Lucas Educational Foundation, and Pat Harder. (*Edutopia,* Fall 2003), 15.

32. Dresang, *op. cit,* 29.

33. N. Paley (1990). Cited in Eliza T. Dresang, *Radical Change* (New York: H.W. Wilson Company, 1999).

34. *Children's Software and New Media Revue,* May/June 2003, 8.

35. Isabel Beck and Margaret McKeown, "Conditions of Vocabulary Acquisition." In M. L. Kamil, P. B. Mosenthal, and P. D. Pearson (Eds.), *Handbook of Reading Research* (Mahwah, NJ: Lawrence Erlbaum, 1991) 789–814.

36. Shaywitz, *op. cit.,* 140.

37. Julie M. Wood, Can Software Support Children's Vocabulary Development? *Language Learning & Technology,* Vol. 5, No. 1, 2002.

38. D. E. Freeman and Y. S. Freeman, *Teaching Reading in Multilingual Classrooms* (Portsmouth, NH: Heinemann 2000).

39. Steven Stahl, "To Teach a Word Well: A Framework for Vocabulary Instruction." *Reading World,* 24(3), 1985, 16–27; Steven Stahl "Three Principals of Effective Vocabulary Instruction." *Journal of Reading,* 29, 1986, 662–68.

40. William E. Nagy and Richard C. Anderson. "How Many Words Are There in Printed School English?" *Reading Research Quarterly,* 19, 1984, 304–30.

41. Jeanne Chall and Catherine E. Snow, "Families and Literacy: The Contribution of Out-of-School Experiences to Children's Acquisition of Literacy." A final report to the National Institute of Education, 1982.

42. Cited in Marjorie Y. Lipson and Karen K. Wixson, *Assessment & Instruction of Reading and Writing Disability.* (New York: Harper Collins, 1991).

43. Dorothy Grant Hennings, "Contextually Relevant Word Study: Adolescent Vocabulary Development Across the Curriculum." *Journal of Adolescent & Adult Literacy,* Nov. 2000, Vol. 44, Issue 3.

44. In creating this synthesis I drew heavily upon these sources: James F. Bauman and Edward J. Kame'enui, "Research on Vocabulary Instruction: Ode to Voltaire," In James Flood, J. M. Jensen, Diane Lapp, and James R. Squire (eds.), *Handbook of Research on Teaching the English Language Arts* (New York: Macmillan, 1991); Isabel Beck, Margaret McKeown, and R. C. Omanson, "The Effects and Uses of Diverse Vocabulary Instructional Techniques." In Margaret G. McKeown and Mary E. Curtis (eds.), *The Nature of Vocabulary Acquisition* (Hillsdale, NJ: Erlbaum, 1987); Marjorie Y. Lipson and Karen K. Wixson, *Assessment & Instruction of Reading and Writing Disability* (New York: Harper, 1991); William E. Nagy, *Teaching Vocabulary to Improve Reading Comprehension.* (Urbana, IL: ERIC Clearinghouse on Reading and Communication Skills and the National Council of Teachers of English, 1998); and Steve Stahl and M. Fairbanks, "The Effects of Vocabulary Instruction: A Model-based Meta-analysis." *Review of Educational Research,* 56, 1986, 72–110. In addition a version of these guidelines appeared in the previously cited, Wood, "Can Software Support Children's Vocabulary Development?"

45. William E. Nagy and Patricia A. Herman. "Breadth and Depth of Vocabulary Knowledge: Implications for Acquisition and Instruction. In Margaret G. McKeown and Mary E. Curtis (eds.), *The Nature of Vocabulary Acquisition* (Hillsdale, NJ: Erlbaum, 1987), 19–35.

46. Described in Karen Bromley, *Stretching Students' Vocabulary,* (New York, NY: Scholastic, 2002).

47. Julie M. Wood and Nell K. Duke. "Inside 'Reading Rainbow': A Spectrum of Strategies for Promoting Literacy." *Language Arts, 74,* February, 1997, 101.

48. *Ibid.*

49. Sharon Taberski, "Fact & Fiction Read Aloud," *Instructor,* March 2001, 24.

50. National Assessment of Educational Progress, *www.nces.ed.gov/nationalreportcard.*

51. James Cummins, *Empowering Minority Students,* 1989. (Sacramento, CA: California Association for Bilingual Education).

52. Jeanne Chall, Vicki Jacobs, and L. Baldwin. *The Reading Crisis: Why Poor Children Fall Behind* (Cambridge, MA: Harvard University Press, 1990).

53. Tina Blythe and Associates, *The Teaching for Understanding Guide* (San Francisco: Jossey-Bass, 1998), xi.

54. Adapted from Tina Blythe and Associates, *op. cit.,* 105.

55. Two excellent books about TfU are Tina Blythe and Associates' *The Teaching for Understanding Guide* (1998) and M. Stone Wiske's *Teaching for Understanding* (1998). Each one address issues related to implementing TfU in the classroom, and offers case studies documenting the process.

56. Julie M. Wood, "Go Right to the Source!" *Instructor Magazine,* Scholastic, November/December 2000, 71.

57. Roberta Furger, "The Write Stuff," *Edutopia,* Fall 2003, 5.

58. Richard Marius, *A Writer's Companion,* 2d ed. (New York: McGraw Hill, 1991), 14.

59. "NAEP writing test shows modest gain." In *The Reading Teacher* (Newark, DE: The International Reading Association), 3. See also *nces.ed.gov/nationsreportcard/writing/results2002* for more information.

60. *Reading Today,* June/July 2003, 4. "The Neglected 'R' Report" is available at *www.writingcommission.org.* Or, you can order a printed copy by calling (212) 713-8240 and asking for number 997548.

61. Edward B. Fiske, *Smart Schools, Smart Kids* (New York: Simon & Schuster, 1991) 157.

62. See also Julie M. Wood. (Summer 2000). "A Marriage Waiting to Happen: Computers and Process Writing." Education Development

Center's website: *www.edtechleaders.org/Resources/Readings/Upper ElemLiteracy/ Wood_ComputersWriting.htm*

63. *Reading Today,* December 2000/January 2003, 10.

64. R. C. Anderson, P. T. Wilson, and L. G. Fielding. "Growth in Reading and How Children Spend Their Time Outside School." *Reading Research Quarterly, 23,* 1988, 285–303.

65. Marilyn J. Adams, *op. cit.,* 5.

66. Jay R. Campbell, Catherine M. Hombo, and John Mazzeo, NAEP 1999 *Trends in Academic Progress: Three Decades of Student Performance,* U.S. Department of Education (Washington, DC: National Center for Education Statistics, 2000). Also available at *http://nces.ed. gov/nationsreportcard*

67. Cited by Jim Trelease in The Read-Aloud Handbook, 5th ed. (New York: Penguin, 2001), 1–2.

68. Cited by Melissa Clark, Pilar Guzman, Roopika Nayar, and Craig Ofman in Real Simple, August 2003, 140.

3

Lessons from the Reading Lab for Teachers and Students

I am part of all that I have met…
—*Ulysses*, Alfred Lord Tennyson

What type of literacy gains can you anticipate when you integrate telecommunications tools into your reading and language arts curricula? In this section I will show you by zeroing in on two of the essential literacy skills discussed in Part 2: writing (number 6) and motivation (number 7). I hope that this glimpse inside the Jeanne Chall Reading Laboratory, which takes place during the 1999–2000 academic year, when I served as its director, will inspire you to design *your own innovation*. As you will see, the teachers I worked with and I didn't have state-of-the-art technology, nor did all the Lab teachers embrace new tools for learning, at least not at first. Read on.

The Setting

A city with just over 100,000 inhabitants, Cambridge is situated on the Charles River, across from Boston. It first developed as a publishing center for the colonies in the seventeenth century because it had one of the first printing presses. Over the centuries, Cambridge became home to many scholars, writers, reformers, and intellectuals. During the American Revolution the patriots established their military headquarters in Cambridge, in the aftermath of the dramatic events at Lexington and Concord. In fact, George Washington took command of the Continental Army on the Cambridge Common, just a block away from the scene I describe. Henry Wadsworth Longfellow, Oliver Wendall Holmes, and Julia Child have also lived here, to name just a few well-known residents who have left an indelible mark.

Since 1636, Cambridge has been the home of Harvard College, the first American college, which began with an enrollment of 12 young men and a strong religious leaning. Today, 350-plus years later, Harvard University enrolls over 18,000 degree candidates.[1]

The Lab as a Force for Social Good

The Lab was located in the basement of Larsen Hall, an imposing brick building situated on Appian Way, a quaint, brick-lined street tucked between two main thoroughfares—Garden and Brattle Streets. The image many people have of Harvard as a Boston Brahmin institution, with well-born but often mediocre students, and a snobbish outlook, may have been accurate many years ago.[2] However, the GI Bill of Rights, student radicalism of the 1960s, and the economic upsets of the 1970s brought about drastic changes, in the institution. Under the leadership of two recent presidents; Derek Bok (1971–1991) and Neil Rudenstine (1991–2001), Harvard developed a "new, more worldly belief in diversity, broadened-access, and the university as a force for social good."[3] Eager to cast aside its patrician image, over the past three decades Harvard has enlarged its focus and set about enacting social policy, attracting faculty and students from all over the world. Today it offers a "proliferation of activities that stretch the envelope of what a university is supposed to do."[4] The vision for the future of Harvard, as former President Rudenstine described it, is one of a university "helping to address the most important problems that confront the nation and the larger world."[5]

My story begins on a crisp day early in the fall. The leaves are just beginning to turn golden. They fairly glow against a clear blue sky, as electric as a painting by van Gogh.

Down in the Lab, preparations for students' arrival are underway. The students who attend the Lab's instructional program were selected through an application and selection process. That is, a parent or teacher applied to the Lab on a student's behalf; tuition is free. The previous summer I had reviewed the application forms, prioritizing students according to their learning issues and whether I thought the Lab placement could serve them well.

Today I count eight teachers, between their early 20s and late 40s, each caught up in the ebb and flow of the midweek afternoon. The group represents roughly half of the teachers who are enrolled in a course called "Theory and Practice of Reading." Most teachers in the course plan to become certified reading specialists. Others may decide to work in less traditional educational settings such as museums or nonprofit research organizations (think tanks).

The children teachers work with face serious challenges. Former director Vicki Purcell-Gates succinctly captures the types of learners we've come to know over the years. She summarizes:

> . . . first and second graders who still have not focused on print and who exhibit early emergent literacy behaviors, ninth graders who cannot read beyond memorized Dr. Seuss books and who cannot write more

than a few sentences with unconventional spelling and punctuation, seventh graders who like to read Judy Blume books but cannot comprehend their social studies texts, developmentally delayed ten-year-olds with neurologically-based motor and perceptual problems who have yet to read or write anything beyond letters and simple words in a workbook, and second-language learners, from both literate and nonliterate homes, who are trying to learn both the language of the United States and the language of books.[6]

Similar to the students Purcell-Gates describes, we have older students who may not have ever read a chapter book on their own, let alone an entire chapter in their science textbook; middle-grade students who wish they could read the books the other kids in their class are reading but who lack the necessary decoding skills and fluency to do so. We also have primary-level students who still have difficulty with sound/symbol relationships. Two students are second language learners; others have been diagnosed as learning disabled and/or speech delayed. All but a few struggle with expressing their ideas in writing.

Unique as each of the students is, a careful analysis of data collected about them over an eight-year period reveals two shared qualities. First, many emphatically do not view reading and writing as interesting or enjoyable activities. And second, most students do not perceive themselves as readers and writers. Those activities are for other children. Many of our students have effectively dropped out of what reading expert Frank Smith calls "The Literacy Club"; they don't identify with readers and writers in their social world.[7] To Smith's thinking, full membership in the Club is the ultimate purpose of schooling. These are the children who "don't do school."

THE TEACHING FELLOWS

This afternoon I position myself in the middle of the action. Julie Park, one of the Teaching Fellows (TFs) shoots me a discrete "I-think-I'm-going-crazy" look as three teachers ask her questions at the same time. Julie possesses a miniaturist's eye for detail. She is as fluent in ancient Greek culture as she is knowledgeable about Harry Potter and Hogwarts Academy. Today Julie meets with a teacher who is concerned about her student's aversion to writing *anything* down on paper.

Julie would often encourage new teachers by remarking, "The Lab is an amazing place. You have the luxury of working with one child. Finding the most effective ways to help him become a better reader and writer is an intellectual puzzle for you to figure out over the course of one or two semesters." Furthermore, she'd point out, "You'll never have that opportunity again!"

Natalie LaCroix-White is also a TF in the Lab. Natalie graduated with a master's degree from the Language and Literacy Department the year before Julie. Since leaving the Ed School, she has been a first-grade teacher in a suburb of Boston. Her first-grade classroom has become well-known in the area. She helped teachers select books carefully, making sure to provide the right measure of challenge. (Although TFs are typically drawn from the graduate student population, this particular year it made more sense to enlist recent graduates who were practicing teachers.)

BEHIND THE SCENES AT THE LAB

Our main work surface, a well-worn table, is strewn with children's books and notebooks. Our students begin to arrive, and I enter the teaching area of the Lab to observe sessions. The tools of the trade are scattered about. They're not all that different from what you'd find in typical elementary and middle-grade classrooms across America. Bookcases are placed together to form an L-shaped library area. Most books are in plastic bins, sorted by a combination of genre and grade level (e.g., "Easy Poetry," "Intermediate-Level Mysteries"). Books such as *Llama in Pajamas* and *Ruby Bridges* are displayed on top of the bookcases.

Previously this fall I arranged for students to have their own email accounts. For reasons of safety, children can access their accounts in the Lab only after three adults have previewed messages. The cycle went like this: Students' mail was delivered directly to teachers. Once teachers received messages intended for their students, they read them and copied them to their Teaching Fellow and me so that we, too, could read them. Today eight-year-old "Cecily Salamander"[8] (a.k.a. Jackie) opens her email account. Her eyes scan the screen and then light up. Someone has sent her an email message.

Dear Cecily,
I read your story and I liked it very much.
I hope you write another one.
Samantha

After conferring with her teacher, Cecily writes back:

Where are you from? I am going to have a new story on my page. It is going to be about a salamander and a lizard. They are going to find a magical ring. What school do you go to? Write back soon.
Cecily Salamander

At a nearby table, twelve-year-old "SpicyTaco" (a.k.a. Richard) collaborates with his teacher on a K-W-L chart for Quidditch, an imaginary sport that figures prominently in the *Harry Potter* series.[9] SpicyTaco is creating the chart in preparation for writing an expository essay about Quidditch. Under the "What I Learned" column Richard writes:

Quidditch is a game played high up in the air with players flying around on brooms. It's like a combination of soccer and basketball and a little of hockey. For more information read the Harry Potter books or check out our map on Quidditch (SEE BELOW!).

On a second computer, ten-year-old "Spike" (a.k.a. Ashley) clicks onto her personal Web page. Her story, "If You Give a Dog a Dessert," has just been posted on her personal Web page by the web master. The circular story, modeled on books such as the popular *If You Give a Mouse a Cookie,* by Laura Joffe Numeroff, represents a major accomplishment for Spike, whose fine motor problems make writing with pencil and paper extremely slow and tedious. In fact, being a published author on the Web becomes a defining moment for Spike—it marks the beginning of her perception of herself as a *real* writer.

I'll describe Lab students' progress later in this section. Essentially each child readily learned to use new technologies in new ways; opportunity led to invention. And in so doing, students became more accomplished readers and writers. They also joined the Literacy Club.

JEANNE CHALL'S LEGACY

> *Education is not the filling of a pail, but the lighting of a fire.*
> —William Butler Yeats

The Jeanne Chall Reading Lab has achieved fame as a training ground for hundreds of teachers and reading specialists since 1966, when it invited participation from the Cambridge community. The major force behind the Lab was Dr. Chall herself, who figured prominently as one of the foremost educators and researchers in the second half of the twentieth century. Chall conceived of a place where teachers could be trained and children with reading difficulties, particularly those in low-income settings, could receive free instruction. Data from instructional sessions often became the focus of Chall's research.

Chall was among the first researchers to conceptualize learning to read as a series of developmental stages. Her book *Stages of Reading Development* (1983) became a classic in the field, mapping out the stages children progress through as they learn to read.

A Brief Summary of Chall's Stages of Reading Development

"The reading of the stumbling beginner is not the reading of the fluent third grader nor of the skilled college freshman," explained Chall. "It takes most people about twenty years to reach the highest stage of reading development. Some people reach it much faster, others take longer," she remarked in *Stages of Reading Development* (p. 7).

Briefly, a summary of the five stages Chall advanced follows.

- *Stage* 1 in grades 1–2.5, in which the reader is concerned with breaking the code of print;
- *Stage* 2 in grades 2 and 3, characterized by confirmation, fluency and "ungluing" from print. During this stage students enjoy reading and rereading familiar books;
- *Stage 3* is split into two phases. In *Stage* 3A, students in grades 4–6 (approximately), read for a variety of purposes (e.g., to find information for class assignments or to pursue their own topics of interest). In *Stage* 3B, middle school students can synthesize information from multiple sources; they also develop their own preferences.
- Students at *Stage 4*, roughly high school age, are capable readers who can enjoy reading and apply it to academic work involving critical analysis of texts.
- In *Stage* 5, college students gain "a world view." At this stage, readers, often motivated by their own tastes and preferences, focus on learning to construct knowledge on an abstract plane.

Chall's most widely discussed work was arguably *Learning to Read: The Great Debate* (1967) because of its controversial nature. In this volume Chall synthesized the available research about phonics and literature-based reading instruction. During the era of "the reading wars," this work was often cited as a polemical treatise in favor of teaching phonics. However, many believe this to be an inaccurate and misinformed interpretation. *The Great Debate*, in fact, advocated many ideas associated with the whole language movement. For example, Chall suggested that children read books in lieu of worksheets when not working directly with the teacher. She also advocated incorporating writing into reading, a practice that's also aligned with a whole language philosophy.

Another of Chall's books, *The Reading Crisis: Why Poor Children Fall Behind*, which she collaborated on with others, influenced a generation of reading professionals. Other legacies that bear Chall's unique stamp include the classic children's television programs she took delight in consulting on, *Sesame Street* and *The Electric Company*. Harvard was Chall's intellectual base for more than thirty years, until she died in 1999 at age 78.

Dr. Chall and Dr. Seuss

Oh, the places you'll go, as Theodor Geisel, more commonly known as Dr. Seuss, might say... A little known fact about Dr. Jeanne Chall is that Chris Cerf, one of the creative forces behind the educational television series, *Between the Lions*, was a former student of hers. Chris' father was Bennett Cerf, who owned Random House Publishers. Years ago Dr. Chall had lamented to Bennett and his wife, Phyllis, that few children's trade books were written with the 200 words students need to know; those books that did feature these target words weren't written by top children's authors. The Cerfs responded by contacting Dr. Seuss, inviting him to try his hand at writing texts that emphasized high-utility words. Thus, a series of easy readers was launched, all edited by Phyllis. The centerpiece of the series was *The Cat in the Hat*.[10]

TWENTY-FIRST CENTURY LITERACIES AND STRUGGLING READERS AND WRITERS

Winged words make their own spiral; caught in them, we are lost, or found...
—H. D. Doolittle

In carrying out Chall's mission, how much progress could the Literacy Lab expect to make in a school year? Our records of student assessments, using both formal (standardized tests) and informal measures (e.g., writing samples), showed that students typically thrived academically in the Lab, demonstrating important gains in many critical areas.[11] Many learned to become strategic readers, not just as readers of fiction, but in all types of genres. They began to devour magazines like *Ranger Rick*, *TIME for Kids*, and *Sports Illustrated for Kids*, for their crisp writing style and contemporary appeal. They also racked up several titles in the American Girl series, and at least the first Harry Potter book.[12] Middle-grade students often became big Roald Dahl fans when they discovered *James and the Giant Peach* and *Mathilde*. Other popular authors included Patricia Polocco, R. L. Stien, Katherine Paterson, Jon Scieszka, Arnold Lobel, and Faith Ringgold.

Many children were surprised to discover that writing could help them express what they knew or what they believed. Having a ready audience for their work, via the Internet, gave them an impetus for writing a report, posting a book review, or displaying a poster of a Venn diagram depicting the similarities and differences between lizards and salamanders. Over time, children cultivated visitors to their own web pages and contributed to popular existing sites, such as Amazon.com; they become members of a literate community.

THE COMPUTER MINILAB

Our minilab was modest. We had just three computers, none state-of-the-art. We had the usual tangle of wires, scattered headsets scattered, rack of CD-ROMs (holding titles such as *American Girl*, *Tenth Planet*, and *National Geographic Atlas of the World*), and basic printers.

Technological Fluency

Remarkably, all the children in the Lab, in spite of having come from a wide range of schools, were computer literate. Naturally there are socioeconomic implications in knowing one's way around computers. Simply stated, very poor children often lack exposure to computers and thus are shortchanged on multiple levels. Computers are now so ubiquitous in everyday life, that to be inexperienced in using them as thinking tools is to be out of step with most of society. Children of all races, classes, and cultures need to be technologically fluent. "It is widely recognized that advanced information technologies are increasingly important as tools of education, socialization, and the acquisition of work skills," observed William Julius Wilson of Harvard's John F. Kennedy School of Government, who studies the urban poor. "For those with access to training and education, they are a key to opportunity. For those deprived of access and training, advanced information technologies can become barriers to social mobility," Wilson continues.[13] Our students were fortunate. Each had at least some degree of access to computers at school and/or at home.

Few would disagree with the notion that children are by nature facile with computers and other gadgets. Among our students, seven-year-old Jeffrey was as much at home with a mouse, keyboard, and pull-down menus as thirteen-year-old Jonathan. Every child knew how to call up the Lab's home page on the Internet and access each other's work as well as their own. The youngest children had memorized the URLs for the best Pokemon and reptile websites, while the older boys knew how to access their favorite preoccupation—the World Wrestling Foundation (WWF). The older girls were attracted to websites where they could find information about their hobbies, such as drawing horses or learning about rainforest animals or favorite authors.

A few children reported using America Online's Instant Messenger feature (IM) at home, which allows people to write quick, abbreviated messages to each other. One reason IM is so popular is because users are not limited to one-to-one conversations; instead they can virtually chat with any and all of their friends who happen to be logged on at the same moment. Typically, messages are laced with an entire lexicon of abbreviated phrases. ROFL is *Rolling on the Floor Laughing,* for example. ICU stands for *I see you.*

> *I believe that the new language, if you will, is a real way for kids to begin to understand how the English language is alive and kicking.*
> —Dana Clark, D. W. Daniel High School, Central, South Carolina[14]

Instant Messaging Phrases

afk	away from keyboard
j/k	just kidding
sup	what's up?
b4	before
aamof	as a matter of fact
l8r	later
brb	be right back

tc	take care
ttyl	talk to you later
ianalb	I am not a lawyer, but. . .

For many more abbreviations (and emoticons; you know, those faces made with keyboard symbols to express emotions), see web pages by Jim Shook:

www.net-comber.com/acronyms.html and *www.net-comber.com/emoticons.html*

If you were to observe the minilab over time, you'd see students experience the pleasure of printing their original stories and reports. You'd hear them reading email messages out loud. You'd see them respond to messages sent by visitors to their web pages from close to home or a continent away.

A word of caution, though. As you are well aware, chat rooms can be dangerous. Also, the Internet abounds with inappropriate websites. Students might stumble onto some of these nefarious sites quite innocently. For example, if children misspell a name such as Britney Spears, or of a popular Disney character during an Internet search, they can accidentally find themselves on an X-rated site; once there, students can become "mousetrapped" (i.e., no easy exit). It's up to us to carefully brief students about the Internet safety guidelines and then be hypervigilant whenever they are using telecommunications tools in our presence. To learn more about Internet safety, check out these two excellent publications:

- "The Parents' Guide to the Internet," available online through The Children's Partnership at *www.childrenspartnership.org/bbar/pbpg.html*

- "Tips for Keeping Your Children Safe Online" (*PC World*) at *www.idg.net/go.cgi?id=15757*

PUBLISHING STUDENT WORK

Publishing student work can be one of the best ways for you to help children realize that writing is an intensely communicative act. Fortunately in today's world you can extend your reach beyond school corridors, local newspapers, and magazines like *Stone Soup* that publish student work. By taking advantage of the Internet, you can give young authors an unparalleled way to share their work; more remarkably, students can receive a response in a matter of seconds.

Having Students Share Their Work with a Wide Audience

Looking for avenues that invite students to publish their work? If so, you're in luck. Many websites invite students to submit their original work. These four can get you started.

- **Candlelight Stories** (See *www.candlelightstories.com*)
- **Kidscribe,** particularly for ESL students (See *web2.airmail.net/def*)
- **Young Writer** (See *www.mystworld.com/youngwriter*)
- **Young Author's Magazine Program** (See *www.yam.regulus.com*)

First Foray into Cyberspace

What if instead of publishing their original work on the established websites, mentioned previously, students could post their writing on a personalized website? Would such a venue boost students' motivation to write and polish their work? I thought it was worth a try. But although products like DreamWeaver and HomePage make creating a web page pretty easy today, just a few years ago it was more complicated. I advertised for technical help. Enter David Grogan, a master's degree student who had a background in computer sciences from a college in Glasgow, Scotland. He and I soon mapped out what we believed to be the most important aspects of a website for Lab students.

Design Notes for You to Use in Building a Website

Where to begin? I offer these guidelines, which David and I developed, as a blueprint for those of you who are interested in getting started. How can you adapt them to meet the needs of *your* students and *your* teaching philosophy?

1. Children will have their own individual web page.
   - Each personal web page will become a vehicle for students to introduce themselves through a brief autobiographical sketch

and a self-portrait; these original pieces will enable them to establish their own identity on the Web.[15]

- We will take advantage of the hypertext environment by creating links to the subjects children wrote about in their autobiographies. For example, a reference to having been born in Mexico can be linked to child-friendly information about that country.

- We will also highlight children's hobbies and interests. If they're Pokemon fanatics, we'll add links to the best Pokemon sites; if they're keen on horses, we'll add links to interesting sites about different breeds of horses, some of which have been created by children.

2. Children will be able to publish their original work.
   - Each personal website will have a section where children can post their polished compositions and illustrations. A "Work of the Week" link will spotlight a particular student's work.
   - Children's postings will not only serve as an electronic portfolio, but will also allow kids to publish many different types of compositions including poems, book reviews, scientific reports about subjects like salamanders, and biographical sketches of favorite sports heroes.

My Links

- All About Football
- Basketball Mania
- Our Harry Potter Pages: Edleston, England
- ROC's Quadditch Fan Site
- U.S. Soccer Federation
- The Wonderful World of Harry Potter

SpicyTaco's links from his website

3. Children need be able to transcend local boundaries.
   - Interactive components will be essential. We will build in email accounts to capitalize on the extended readership of children's stories and information pieces. That is, by using a

simple mouse-click a reader in Canada can access a child-author and respond to his writing, hobbies, or artwork.

- We will have a "Guest Book" in which visitors can enter their names, locations, and email addresses along with a greeting. This will help us develop a sense of our audience as the project evolves.
- We will feature two ongoing galleries. One will feature book reviews submitted by our students as well as readers from all over; the second will offer a list of electronic resources related to literacy development.[16]

In our real-world environment I posted two maps—one of the United States and another of the world, to help us keep track of our correspondents. The simple act of writing "Karen Duke, East Lansing, Michigan" on a tag, and then positioning it the map lent authenticity to the project. Over time, our pin map showed correspondents as near as Cape Cod, Massachusetts, and as far away as New Zealand. The pin map also lent itself to geography lessons. For instance, a student might look up a location such as Maui or Montana in a traditional atlas and then locate it on the wall map. As email poured in, the maps became important tools.[17]

Over time, publishing on the Web and corresponding with *todo el mundo* via email—two complementary processes—gained momentum. Truth be told, not everyone who wrote to us discovered our website through serendipity. We contacted friends and acquaintances all over the world and persuaded them to write to our students. Not only did we cast our net over as many continents as possible, we also targeted friends who were involved in doing "cool things." One teacher, for example, contacted a diver she knew from the Boston Aquarium. His job was to feed the fish and monitor the health and behavior of all the creatures in the huge multistoried tank of the aquarium. Other interesting correspondents included a soccer coach, a cartoonist, a gymnast, and several space scientists.[18]

Connecting with Keypal Exchange Agencies

Are you interested in engaging your students in a keypal exchange? If so, two of the best resources are:

- Rigby Heinemann Keypals List. (See *www.reedbooks.com.au/keypals/default.asp*)
- ePals (See *www.epals.com*)

VIDEOTAPING LAB SESSIONS

In addition to the website project, I also piloted a method for capturing and recording children's and teachers' interactions at the computer. The traditional problem is this: Videotaping or photographing children at the computer always involves a trade-off. Either you can focus on the child's face and miss what's happening online, or you can focus on the computer screen and find that you've only captured the back of people's heads. Neither option is very satisfying. Inspired by the ideas of my colleague, Bart Pisha at the Center for Applied Special Technologies, I asked an inventor to build a mirror that I could attach to the top of the computer monitor. The mirror we designed was approximately one foot high and three feet wide. It sat on a platform that allowed us to angle it both up and down and swivel it from side to side. Long red-and-black suspenderlike straps allowed us to firmly secure the mirror to the monitor.

I highly recommend this mirror device to other researchers; it dramatically improved the data collection process. Although distracting at first, I was able to capture interactions between teachers and students with many more dimensions than would have been possible otherwise.

LESSONS FROM THE LAB

The biggest surprise was that students stayed close to home with their email exchanges. I had been thinking along the lines of Cummins and Sayers' *Brave New Schools* and their success with international projects. The people they wrote about were enthusiastic writers within a global community. Although a few of our students' email exchanges had an international flavor (as with Medo and his messages to relatives in Lebanon), most did not. To quote the legendary former Speaker of the House, Tip O'Neill, "All politics is local." Jaime, for example, wrote to his mother and her colleagues who worked in a high-tech company. James wrote to his father at work. Jackie exchanged ideas about books with the reading specialist at her school, just a few blocks from the Lab.

James' case was especially interesting. He was uncomfortable writing to strangers and preferred to restrict his socializing to people he knew. As his teacher explained, "He likes sending and getting email, but only from people he knows. Maybe he's had bad responses. He *is* anxious to get messages from his father." When it came to posting work on the Web, Sandy observed of James, "It was a struggle to get him to put up work at first. At first he was excited about posting his World

Wrestling Federation (WWF) project on the web, but then he expressed anxiety about [the possibility of] receiving too many responses."[19]

I learned some very important lessons that year; the following three stand out in my mind. I hope they will shed light on your own teaching—where you've been and where you want to go next.

Lesson 1: Students, if given a bit of latitude, will appropriate electronic media in ways that fulfill their own academic and psychological needs and desires.

Lesson 2: Never underestimate the power of telecommunications to help students establish their own *voice* as writers.

Lesson 3: Email correspondence can have a profound impact on a young writer's emerging sense of audience.

Lesson 1: Students, if given a bit of latitude, will appropriate electronic media in ways that fulfill their own academic and psychological needs and desires.

By way of illustration, here is the story of nine-year-old Jackie, one of the students in the Lab. She explained her new computer identity in an email message: "My name is not really Cecily. I have a friend named Cecily, though. I just use 'Cecily Salamander' as a computer name." (Jackie's fondness for Salamanders led her to select this word as part of her pseudonym.)

Jackie's Lab experience demonstrated how targeted instruction in reading and writing, in parallel with many opportunities to express herself using media, can promote literacy development. In preparation for writing this book, I asked Jackie's teacher, Kristin Kellogg Valdmanis, to write a case study describing Jackie's progress over the course of two semesters. In short, Jackie went from reading and writing below grade level to becoming an avid reader of grade-level trade books (fiction and nonfiction) and a skilled writer in a variety of text genres, such as scientific reports, letters, and book reviews. As she remarked to her teacher with downcast eyes, "Yeah, I used to have this tutor 'cause I didn't know how to read and stuff." To understand Jackie's progress, I have drawn heavily on Kristin's account.[20]

Jackie's Story

Jackie is a teacher's dream. She is a diligent student who does just about everything that is asked of her with few complaints. She is friendly, polite, and generally quite happy-go-lucky. But when Jackie talks candidly about school, she reveals that her good-natured facade is actually masking a deep insecurity related to a lack of self-esteem.

Jackie's main problem is that although she is a capable student who can do age-appropriate work, she does not view herself as a smart kid. Rather, Jackie is convinced that she is "dumb," especially compared to two exceptionally high-achieving best friends whom she has known since early childhood. This negative self-image greatly contributes to a less than enthusiastic attitude about school and schoolwork, particularly reading and writing. Even though Jackie is completing her work in school, she isn't putting her all into her assignments; her half-hearted effort is beginning to take its toll on her grades and scores.

When she arrives at the Harvard Literacy Lab, Jackie brings with her this self-doubt and a waning interest in intellectual pursuits. As Jackie's Lab teacher, I [Kristin] am charged with bolstering her self-esteem in addition to helping her improve her reading and writing skills. I use a variety of methods to reach these goals, but ultimately it was the creation of an alternative computer identity that helps Jackie begin to take some important academic risks, eventually challenging and reshaping her view of herself as a student.

Though unsure of herself as a student, Jackie is certain that she is a "cool kid" who is in touch with the teenage trends that rule the media. She distinguishes herself from other children her age in the Lab by adopting a sophisticated, mature appearance and persona (although she is a petite child who looked very young). This sophistication rarely appeared in her writing, however. Rather, her early compositions are childlike and simplistic, often giving the reader the impression that they were composed by an emergent writer.

Assessing Jackie's Writing Skills Jackie's composition abilities are quite weak at the beginning of the fall semester. One of her first pieces of fiction revealed that she is not a confident, fluent writer. Below is a copy of her text, as she wrote it.

Freckals and the Pet

One day Freckals was lonely. He had know freinds to play with. So he had a idia that he could have a pet. So he drove his car to the pet store. Whene he got in the pet store he looked arouned. He saw a cat that was realy cute. It was a baby cat. He liked it so much he bout it. He plade wiht it every day. So he lived happly ever after THE End.

Spelling, word choice, and story development are clearly challenging for Jackie. She overuses simple connectives such as "so," making the piece repetitive and formulaic. Additionally, her vocabulary is immature, robbing her written work of the sophistication that she prides herself on. Nonfiction writing is also difficult as shown by the following early composition, as she wrote it:

How I Got My Salamanders

One day I was playing with my freind Brittaney. Then he mom asked if I could go with her to New Hampsion. I asked my mom and dad and they said yes So me and Brittaney went to New Hampsion. When we got there we looked for salamanders but we could not fined any. So we unpacked are stuff. and after that we went to bed when we woke up we ate beakfast and we went looking for salamanders in about 1 owr we founded 20. salamanders afte that we went home.

Jackie's tale is just barely held together by a narrative thread that relies on the chronology of events; Jackie simply recalls each event in the order in which it happened. She relies heavily on the simple connectives (so, and) to give the piece coherence. The overall effect of these word choices is to render the story plodding and dull. Further, her story lacks the drama and excitement that usually accompanies a story about a favorite animal.

Online Help for Writers of All Ages

Do you have students like Jackie who struggle with expressing themselves in writing? If so, these resources can help.

- How to write a five-paragraph essay (See: *www.geocities.com/Athens/Parthenon/9502/essay.html*)
- Help with writing a biography (See *www.bham.wednet.edu/bio/biomaker*.htm)

  Adolescents can seek help from these resources

- Purdue University Online Writing Lab (See *Owl.english.purdue.edu*)
- The McCallie School Writing Center (See *Blue.mccallie.org/wrt_ctr/*)

Improving Jackie's Writing Skills To help Jackie improve her writing, I [Kristin] introduce the writing process (brainstorming, writing, revising, editing, and sharing) to Jackie to give her a concrete strategy for composing written pieces. I particularly stress the revising and editing phase as a way to encourage Jackie to focus her energies on making her story clear as well as interesting to the reader. I also encourage her to correct spelling, punctuation, and capitalization errors. But at first, Jackie is resistant; she doesn't want to spend time revising and editing her work. I speculate that she is ambivalent about publishing her writing.

For security reasons, all students are required to select pseudonyms. Jackie chooses the name "Cecily Salamander" for publishing work on her web page and communicating with others via email. Along with her new identity is an opportunity to reinvent herself. She is no longer the "dumb" girl in school. Rather, with her new computer identity, she feels a newfound freedom to write, research, and discuss intellectual topics with relative ease and without the inevitable comparisons to peers.

Creating a Computer Identity Publishing her work online is especially enticing to Jackie because she considers the computer and the Internet to be "cool tools," ones that greatly appeal to the budding teenager inside of her. Children are particularly observant of older siblings, parents, and teachers when these key figures in their lives use the computer. Children love to emulate grown-up behaviors and subsequently delight in using technology.

Similarly, Jackie thinks that using email and designing a web page are indeed grown-up activities. But although she likes to use the computer for fun and entertainment, she is a relative newcomer to the use of technology for academic purposes. Jackie tells Julie Wood that she "just messes around" on the computer at home, playing games and looking up song lyrics. Using the computer for writing and communication are new activities for Jackie, but ones that she warms to because of their sophisticated appeal.

Providing Jackie with a New Forum for Communicating Ideas If the purpose of writing is to communicate ideas, the Internet provides Jackie with the ultimate forum. No longer for her eyes only, or for a select few, Jackie is inspired to concentrate on the mechanics of her compositions; she knows they are bound for the Web where they could be viewed by millions of readers.

When Jackie publishes her first story, "Furry and Sally," on her web page she receives several email messages regarding its quality. The world was watching! After receiving a message from Samantha, a new correspondent, Jackie writes:

Dear Samantha,

Where are you from? I am going to have a new story on my page. It is going to be about a salamander and a lizard. They are going to find a magical ring. What school do you go to? Write back soon.

Cecily Salamander

I coach Jackie in composing this message, encouraging her to ask questions. She is highly motivated to write a well-composed message to Samantha. To my surprise, Jackie even makes sure that she runs the spell checker to avoid broadcasting mistakes to her new e pal.

Jackie Uses the Web to Publish Her Work Jackie begins to chart her email correspondences and place markers on the world map in the Lab. She discovers that people as far away as Colorado and California are reading her work and are clearly enjoying it. In parallel with her growing audience, Jackie's self-esteem improves. (Again, everyone in the Lab worked behind the scenes to cultivate a ready audience for all children's work.) Jackie anxiously checks her email and breaks out in a huge smile when she receives a positive response to one of her stories. She soon carefully writes, revises, and edits another piece, "The Ring." She advertises this story to her many e-pals, becoming in effect her own publicist. Here are several "ads" for her upcoming tale:

> I am having a new story and it is called The Magical Ring. It's about a salamander and a lizard and they find a two rings. They find out it's magical.

> I am writing a new story that is about a salamander and a lizard and they find a magic gold ring. Please read it.

> I also have a new story on my webpage and the name is called The Ring. What character is your favorite in The Ring story? Please write back.

Suddenly Jackie envisions herself as a writer with an interested audience. Instead of shrugging her shoulders and displaying an aloof attitude about sharing her work, Jackie now submits stories regularly to the Lab's web master, Gina, to be published on her page. She loves to check her site to see her new postings; she continues to delight in checking her email to meet her new admirers.

Transfer of Knowledge Jackie's new sophisticated approach to writing is not limited to the Web. She and I [Kristin] are in the practice of using dialog journals as a way to reflect on the books she's read and have conversations about them. In the early fall, Jackie would respond to my questions with one- or two-word answers. While reading Beverly Cleary's *Ramona the Pest*, for example, I asked Jackie to describe her favorite Ramona adventure. She replied, "I like the red boots thing because it was funny." I encourage her to write more elaborate, specific responses, but she is characteristically reluctant and slap-dash. Toward the end of the year, however, she begins to use full sentences and descriptive language. When we read *Mr. Popper's Penguins*, by Richard Atwater, Jackie asks me a series of questions: "Do you think Mrs. Popper is happy about all those penguins in her house? Do you think Mr. Popper will get more and more penguins?" In writing these questions, Jackie demonstrates a growing awareness of audience. She learns to elicit my opinion through asking questions. At last we are having a two-way conversation.

Online Book Reports

Are you interested in having your students apply their writing skills to writing and publishing book reports? If so, check out **KidsReads**, an excellent resource, that invites written submissions, as well as games and activities (e.g., trivia) related to books. Students can also cast their votes for favorite books via an online poll. (See *KidsReads.com*)

Or see popular children's book author, Jon Scieszka's website, **Guys Read,** which is specifically designed to get boys excited about reading. (See *www.penguinputnam.com/static/packages/us/yreaders/guysread/*)

Jackie Uses the Internet as a Research Tool What is *krill*? Jackie's research on penguins leads to this new word related to their diet. Jackie decides to investigate *krill* on the Internet. Together we find a child-friendly site that explains that krill are like small shrimp. Delighted with her new knowledge, Jackie prints out the information and stores it in a special folder full of penguin facts. Interested in sharing her knowledge of penguins, she rejects my idea of writing a report and asks if she may create a game instead. She envisioned a board game that children can play online.

After exploring other games on the Web, specifically the PBS website, Jackie comes up with a plan. She will transform her penguin research into an interactive trivia game. Here is a chance to use all her newly honed compositions skills. She writes a list of penguin trivia questions, directions for the game, and instructions for printing out the game board and dice. Eventually the game is published on her webpage for all her new e-pals to play. Over the next few weeks, Jackie receives an overwhelming number of e-mail messages lauding her penguin knowledge and her game (from friends and family of Lab teachers). Below are several examples:

> I really enjoyed reading your latest work. I had no idea that you were a penguin expert! Now I know who to ask if I have any questions. . . How did you come up with the idea to make a game? It looks like a lot of fun. —Laurie [literacy specialist at Jackie's school]
>
> I saw the game you made about penguins, and I just had to stop and write you a letter. I work for the New England Aquarium, and I got the chance to play with them. I even got to scrub their poop off the rocks. They're pretty crazy birds. I thought your game was really cool. Keep up the good work! — Sean, aquarium diver

Jackie is amazed by her audience's response to her penguin project. "Wow!" she exclaims, her mouth curling up at the edges to form a shy smile. "A lot of people sure do like my game!" Jackie has proof that many different people, some beyond her immediate world, think her work is excellent. She begins to see her abilities in a whole new light.

Tried and True Search Engines

Are you interested in having your students conduct research on the Web? If so, three excellent search engines can help:

1. **Google,** for my money, is the best all-around search engine for finding text and images. (See *www.google.com*)
2. **AltaVista** allows you to search by category. (See *www.altavista.com*)
3. If you're an advanced search engine user, try out **The Neverending Search: Finding the Good Stuff.** It's likely you'll discover search tools you never knew existed—from WiseNut, which can help you narrow down your search, to Pandia Search, a powerful search engine that can help you become a power user of the Internet. (See *joycevalenza.com/*)

> 4. Similar to site 3, above, the **Nueva Library Goal: Research** site helps you and your advanced students fine-tune your information literacy skills; librarians suggest different research strategies depending on your goal. (See *nuevaschool.org/~debbie/library/research/research.html*)

Jackie's Learning Curve During her time in the Lab, Jackie becomes a student in the broadest sense of the word. No longer the "dumb" girl in school, her new computer identity results in the ability to write, research, and discuss intellectual topics with ease. She no longer compares herself unfavorably against her peers. Her progress in the Lab is impressive. She receives high marks on her spring narrative and expository writing assessments, scoring in the medium to high range in all categories, including word choice story development, and grammar—areas that had been weak in the fall.

Perhaps most striking is the fact that by the end of the spring semester, Jackie's informal assessments have improved as well. Specifically, Jackie actively considers her audience when writing. Her book review of Beverly Cleary's *Muggie Maggie* demonstrates how she confidently uses her new skills.

Cecily Salamander Reviews. . .
"Muggie Maggie"
By Beverly Cleary

OH MY GOSH! Did you know that in the book *Muggie Maggie*, a girl in the 3rd grade does not want to write in cursive? When her teacher sends notes to other teachers, Maggie wants to read them, but she does not know how to read cursive. At the end of the book, Maggie teaches herself how to write in cursive. I would recommend this book to anyone. I like this book a lot!

Jackie is inspired to open with the catchy phrase, "OH MY GOSH!" She then proceeds to "talk" to her audience by asking, *"Did you know that in the book* Muggie Maggie, *a girl in the 3rd grade does not want to write in cursive?"* Her use of this rhetorical "hook" suggests that Jackie has advanced into a new phase of writing on the Web. With her increased confidence, Jackie begins appropriating the Web medium for purposes beyond simply publicizing her own work. She routinely devises ways to excite readers about her favorite books.

Create Your Own Classroom Website

Have you ever considered creating your own classroom website to display your students' original compositions? If so, here are award-winning sites for inspiration. (See *teacher.scholastic.com/professional/teachtech/blueribbonsites.htm*)

Also, take advantage of these four time-saving tools.

- **Educational Web Design:** This site not only provides tools but also offers links to treasure troves of free graphics, animations, and sound effects. (See *www.oswego.org/staff/cchamber/webdesign.htm*)
- **iTools HomePage:** Part of Apple's Internet services, free to many Macintosh users. Includes templates, editing tools, hosting. (See *www.apple.com*)
- **SiteCentral:** Web authoring software by Knowledge Adventure, especially well suited for *HyperStudio* projects. (See *www.knowledgeadventure.com*)
- **Scholastic.com:** A user-friendly website creation tool for teachers. (See *teacher.scholastic.com*)

Jackie's case reminds me [Julie Wood] of Sherry Turkle's theory that the computer is *an object that lends itself to appropriation*. The computer offers a mirror that reflects our identity back to us. It allows us to see ourselves anew.[21]

Developing an Online Persona Leads to Improved Writing Jackie indeed began to see herself anew. Over time, she came to realize that she was a skilled reader and writer. Her online persona evolved by urging others to read her stories. She figured out how to entice her readers to play the penguin game she created. Finally, she began urging her audience to read her favorite books. The thread that connected these experiences was the ongoing relationship Jackie established with her readers. And I think it's fair to say that it would have been difficult for her persona as a writer to grow so steadily—and swiftly—without the benefit of modern telecommunications tools.

> *Lesson* 2: Never underestimate the power of telecommunications to help your students establish their own voice as writers.

Voice is writing into which someone has breathed . . . the words go deep."
—Peter Elbow[22]

ESTABLISHING AN INDIVIDUAL VOICE AS A WRITER

How can we help young writers draw upon their individual experiences—and ultimately their worldview—when they sit down to write? How can we help them develop their voice?

What exactly is *voice*? Donald Graves describes voice as the "driving force" that underlies every step of the writing process. "Voice is the imprint of ourselves on our writing."[23] Rather than a mysterious entity, think of voice as a written expression of an author's inner being. We can easily distinguish between a piece written by Mark Twain and another by John Updike because each writer's work is infused with his own distinct spirit. Similarly, there's no mistaking Jane Austin for Danielle Steele.

But often our inner voice doesn't come to us easily as adults. We have an inner critic to contend with. And many of us carry around our own Greek chorus of real and imagined critics that ultimately inhibits the creative process.

Perhaps this is why writing expert Ralph Fletcher argues that we not only need to attune our senses to our inner voice—we must actively pursue it. Fletcher describes the process this way:

> Everyone has an inner voice. But the writer is different from everyone else; the writer listens. She pays attention to it. Frequently she will drop everything to write down whatever it has to say. If the inner voice gets skittish at her approach, she tries sneaking up on it. . . . The writer may not know exactly what the inner voice represents (Unconscious? Superego? Spirit?) but the writer does know one thing: the inner voice is the spokesperson for the inner life.[24]

How attuned are young writers to their inner voices as a reflection of their inner lives? And once they've *heard* their inner voice, how can they capture its spirit in writing?

In this study I observed how email correspondence can jump-start young writers even if their efforts in the past with traditional assignments—science reports, short stories, biographies—have been frustrating. The immediacy of email can assuage young writers' doubts about themselves. It allows for spontaneity and rapid feedback. Email can also introduce children to the idea that many readers are potentially interested in their work. Furthermore, email can help them express themselves in ways that allow their personalities to shine through as they describe a funny incident or explain what makes them curious, or scared, or ecstatic. In essence, email can be an especially powerful medium for children who don't think of themselves as real writers.

Can email have a somewhat remarkable effect on learning? Here is an example to help you decide.

The Case of Eleven-Year-Old "Medo" and How He Became a Writer[25]

> *The desire to write grows with writing.*
> —Erasmus

Everyone knows a child like eleven-year-old "Medo." Medo's difficulties have more to do with "executive functions," or a lack of organizational skills, than with comprehension, decoding, or composing texts. Children like Medo seldom lack in imagination. It's getting the ideas down in a coherent manner that can prove challenging. Here is his story from my perspective [Julie Wood].

"Medo" (his pseudonym) is also a child who, his teacher Emily notes, rarely chooses to read or write for pleasure. Emily observes, "When he does choose a book, he usually chooses it by 'level,' sometimes, length, or story line. . . . He does not like mysteries, but enjoys action/adventure books." As for future aspirations, Emily reports, "Medo told me that he would like to be a chemist when he grows up because he would love to perform experiments."[26]

Ongoing Assessment of Writing Skills Emily administers a narrative writing sample as part of an ongoing assessment process. Using pencil and paper, Medo writes the following story, presented below (in his words):

If I had a purple dragon, I would name it Harry. I don't know why I
Would name it Harry, but I would. . .

We would have a lot of fun together. We might have our own
shows, or mabe we might even go in to the circus. . .

I think it would be fun having a pet dragon. I've always loved
dragons. I think my friends would like my pet dragon just as much
as me.

Here is Emily's written analysis of Medo's writing sample, based on
rubrics provided by the textbook for the course, *Assessment & Instruction of Reading Disability,* by Marjorie Lipson and Karen Wixson[27]:
"Medo did not appear to put forth his best effort on his narrative writing sample. After Medo completed his story, he reported that he was
tired and didn't feel like writing. However, the story was simplistic,
which put Medo in the low and middle skill ranges in the composition
portions of the assessment; it did not tell me much about Medo's potential to write in the narrative genre. No characters were introduced aside
from Medo himself. Neither did he develop his character. His story idea
was interesting, but lacked a clear plot, a setting, and a clear statement
of a problem or resolution."[28]

Organizational Tools for Students

Do some of your students need help organizing their ideas
in written compositions? If so, graphic organizers may
prove to be a powerful ally. Eduscapes and SCORE provide
resources; Education Place and the University of Virginia
provide graphic organizers for you to download.

- **Eduscapes** (See *www.eduscapes.com/tap/topic73.htm*)
- **SCORE** (See *www.sdcoe/k12.ca.us/score/actbank/torganiz.htm*)
- **University of Virginia** (See *curry.edschool.virginia.edu/go/edis771/
  notes/graphicorganizers/graphic/*)

You can also download a tool to help you create your *own* graphic
organizer. (See *teachers.teach-nology.com/web_tools/graphic_org/*)

Medo's expository writing sample is considerably stronger. Emily tells Medo a week in advance that he will be writing an essay and that he can choose the subject. Since he has been studying the Egyptian god, Ra, in school, Medo is able to draw upon his specialized knowledge. He writes the following text with paper and pencil:

> Ra also known as Re, was god of the sun. He was creator of all gods. He was believed to have come out of a lotis flower from the botom of the river of Chaos.
>
> Ra was creator of all the other gods. He created two other gods named Geb and Nut. Then they had Osiris, seth (set), tephnut and Isis. Then Tephnut and Set had Anubis and Osiris and Isis and Horus.
>
> Every day Ra had to fly across the sky as the sun and that was considered as him being born. When the sun set, Ra would die. This would continue throughtout the year. Ra was the most important god.
>
> A scarab (dung beetle) was Ra's symbol. The scarab was also the symbol of life. It would roll a little bit of poop into a ball and laid the egg's into the ball then they would hatch and start a new generation.

Once again Emily analyzes Medo's essay using rubrics developed by Lipson and Wixson. She remarks that although it's clear that Medo knew a great deal about Ra and the mythology surrounding his being, his essay lacks an overall structure. She observes "There is little in the way of an introduction and absolutely no conclusion. His paragraphs were somewhat well structured, however there was little transition between them. . . . His sentences varied in structure, which made his essay more enjoyable to read."[29]

Emily invites Medo to create a personal website, which is a novel experience for him. He quickly warms to the task. A somewhat shy child, when telling his stories Medo will fix you with a grin and launch into one of his humorous tales. He has a keen sense of audience and will look up eagerly at you from beneath a fringe of dark bangs. Did you get it? Medo's humor is reflected in his autobiography.

After Medo introduces himself to the reader through a self-portrait in which he appears as a bemused everyman, he describes his anticipation of the new millennium. His description of the sport he loves—soccer—and how he became a good player, strikes a chord with the young readers we have been cultivating around the world.

Hello. My name is Medo. I was born in Boston, Mass, but my dad was born in Palestine. My family and I are going to Lebanon next year. I think it's going to be very busy because it will be the year 2000, the new millennium.

I have a sister in the tenth grade. She loves to play softball and is pretty good at it. She has to go to a different league because she is too old for her old one. She will miss all of her friends on the team. She had a banquet the same day as my soccer game, so my mom couldn't come to my soccer game, but my dad did.

I have a dog named Molly and a guinea pig named Chip. Molly is a Dalmatian and is two years old. Chip is the guinea pig and is two years old. I feed Chip in the morning. My sister, mom or dad walks Molly in the morning. I have a lot of fun with my pets. I'm getting an iguana when I'm thirteen. I'm not sure what I will name it, but I will figure it out. I can't wait!

I play soccer very well, and I love to do it. It is my favorite sport. I've been playing for three and a half years in a league. My dad used to play when he was little with his friends. My dad's friend introduced me to the game when I was one and a half! He would hold my legs and make them kick a balloon. Then I got the hang of it and was kicking the balloon all by myself.

Online Communication Improves Medo's Writing Shortly after Medo's autobiography is posted on the Lab website, Medo receives this email message from a teacher named Jenny.

Dear Medo,

I am a high school English teacher. I read your story and I liked it very much. I especially liked the part about learning to play soccer when you were so little. The detail about kicking the balloon was really neat. I got a great picture in my head of you as a toddler fumbling with a big balloon. How do Chip and Molly get along? I've always had dogs, but never a guinea pig. Do you have to walk them ever?

Keep up the good work and enjoy your trip to Lebanon!

Sincerely,
Jenny

Here's Medo's response to Jenny, in which we see his offhand humor. He writes:

Dear Jenny,

No, my dog and guinea pig are not really friends. They basically hate each other. Molly terrorizes Chip and would really like to eat him. When he is in his cage she slides in to it with her front paws and scares him so much he has to ron back in to his wooden house.

I do have to walk Molly, but not Chip. I have to walk Molly when I get home from school. Some times I am really tired and I don't want to walk her. So it gets to be a pain when my friends are over. When my friends come over they have to walk her with me. That's not a problem when my friend that has a dog named Zoxie comes over. We walk the dogs together to a field to run around.

Three days later Medo receives a letter from Shelly, an Australian soccer enthusiast. Shelly responds to the specifics of Medo's biography (his upcoming trip to Lebanon) and then offers several conversational hooks (i.e., "Have you ever been to Australia?"). Although it's a relatively short message, it's packed with grist for the writing mill. Shelly also imparts an international flavor to Medo's correspondence as she has lived in both India and Australia and refers to both cultures.

G'day Medo,

I just read your great page and thought I'd drop you a note to say I love soccer too! I hope you have a great time in Lebanon in the year 2000. Have you ever been to Australia? Do you like traveling? I love to!! I was born in the US and moved to India when I was one. I'm currently living in Sydney, Australia, and love it! Keep up the great work with your drawings and writing!

Namaste (Hindi salutation),
Shelly

> ### Focus on Cultural Understandings
>
> Does part of your literacy curriculum include increasing students' cultural awareness? If so, the Kidspin website is for you. Designed for students in grades K–12, Kidspin accepts stories from students around the world; its goal is to open students' eyes to many different cultural perspectives. (See *www.kidspin.com/*)

Medo responds to Jenny's question about whether he'd been to Australia by remarking that although he hasn't, he'd like to go there some day. We see his dry sense of humor emerge when he mentions motion sickness—apparently one of his most enduring memories of the trip he describes. He continues in the spirit of establishing a dialogue by asking Jenny questions.

> No, I have not been to Australia, but I would like to. My friend has an uncle, aunt, and a baby cousin who live in Australia. I have only traveled once to another continent. But when I did, I was only 1 year old. I was very sick, and that is all I need to say about this subject. Anyway I would love to travel to a different place. Have you ever been to Lebanon? Are you excited about the Olympics being in Sydney?
>
> Sincerely,
> Medo

Continuing on the iguana as a pet theme (pun intended), Medo received a message from Terri from Zurich, Switzerland. Terri writes:

> Hey Medo
>
> I came across your homepage today and I was really surprised to read that you have an iguana as a pet! I always thought they were wild animals. In Switzerland, where I am from, people certainly don't have iguanas at home. What can you do with them? Take them for a walk? Stroke them? Play with them? I hope you turn thirteen soon to get your own iguana and to answer my questions!!
>
> Take care and have fun when you go to Lebanon next year!
>
> Terri

Here is Medo's reply, *as he wrote it*

> In America not a lot of people have iguanas that I know of. My cousin used to have two iguanas, three ferrets, one boa constructor, a lot of mice (to feed the snake), and three gerbils. One of my Mom's friend's sons had an iguana and it was potty trained. When it had to go to the bathroom, it would go to the piece of newspaper in the bathroom and go. I'm not sure how they got it to do that, but it was amazing to hear.
>
> Sincerely,
> Medo

Medo's voice in this last message reflects his understanding of his audience. Terri is from Switzerland so Medo couches his reply by first explaining the cultural context of his reply ("In America. . ."). This type of exchange suits Medo's global view, perhaps because he is bicultural and his family's ties to Lebanon are strong.

Composing for an International Audience Emily's case report reveals that Medo loves the fact that his writing appears on the Internet. Because, as noted previously, the Lab teachers and I had an established network of friends and family who visit our Lab website often, Medo receives a flood of responses to his autobiography. Thus encouraged, he is eager to publish more work. Medo, more than any other student, takes delight in writing back to his correspondents. In so doing, he draws upon his writing skills, requiring few reminders to edit his work, mainly because he gets a kick out of using the computer's spell-check.

As for the substance of Medo's writing, Emily remarks, "His letters were very appropriate and full of interesting and fun details about his life and the lives of his friends. In one letter, he told a story about how his mother accidentally killed his pet turtle by trying to force it into hibernation. Emails were probably Medo's favorite part of the Lab."[30]

In summary, Medo appeared to enjoy all that the Web and email exchanges offered him. While he was able to demonstrate a certain level of proficiency in self-expression using traditional tools, Medo hits his stride when he composed for an international audience. The nature of Medo's email exchanges allowed him to be spontaneous. But if, as Henry Miller observed, "You have to write a million words before you find your voice as a writer," then Medo was well on his way, via his email communiqués.

> *Lesson* 3: Email correspondence can have a profound impact on a young writer's emerging sense of audience.

Here is the story of how a Lab student, Richard, a.k.a. "SpicyTaco," learned how to write for an unseen audience. This account draws heavily upon a report by one of Richard's teachers, Nicole Jernée.[31]

"SpicyTaco": Writing for an Unseen Audience

SpicyTaco's Life

My name is SpicyTaco. I was born on March 19, 1987. I was born in Boston. I am the youngest out of my brothers. I am 12 years old, and I go to school in Cambridge. My height is 5'4". I am male, have brown hair and brown eyes. I live in Waltham. It is a very pretty place, but it can get very cold there. I have moved from Cambridge to Waltham. It's a very big difference, but I like where I live. I have two parents. I have two brothers. One is 14, and the other is 20. I am youngest, but it isn't bad being the youngest because you get noticed a lot. I like to play soccer, basketball, and football. These are also my favorite sports.

Richard's Story: A Turning Point for a Reluctant Reader and Writer. Richard is reading in the waiting room of the Lab while waiting for his session. Twice a week, Richard walks to Harvard from his private Catholic school just down the street. It's impossible to miss him as he waits for his session. At age twelve he is the oldest student in the Lab and looks more like a teenager than a seventh grader. By the time he reaches us, his natty school uniform—a navy tie, blue button-down shirt, and navy pants—is in a state of cheerful disarray. As I [Nicole Jernée] glance at the liberated shirttail, untied shoes, rumpled brown hair, and overflowing book bag with homework papers trailing out of semi-zippered compartments, I can't help smiling. He grins back sheepishly, hastily tucking in part of his dress shirt, aware that this sorry state of affairs belies the nuns' careful training.

But what Richard lacks in neatness he more than makes up for in amiability.

Richard is the third and youngest boy in his family. His parents immigrated to the Boston area from Costa Rica. He grew up speaking both Spanish and English.

Richard's difficulties in math, reading, and writing surfaced during the intermediate grades. During these same years, he began to excel in sports, particularly soccer, basketball, and football. He also enjoys a lively social life with his buddies at school.

According to Richard's language arts teacher, he is an engaged learner, but struggles with expressing himself in writing. His sentences are often incomplete, his compositions lack details and supporting evidence. He also finds it hard to organize his ideas in a coherent way. However, none of these difficulties hold him back from socializing with his friends online in AOL chat rooms, when it's finally his turn to use the home computer.

When it comes to computers, Richard is in his element. His competence is one of the first things his fall Lab teacher, Sarah, notices when she begins working with him. He's one of the only students who has keyboarding skills. He knows how to use popular applications such as Microsoft Word. He also demonstrates early on that he is no novice when it comes to using the Internet. He has cultivated favorite sites, and knows how to navigate his way around them. But beyond these competencies, what is most impressive about Richard's involvement with computers is that working on them completely sustains his attention for long stretches of time. And since writers benefit from spending long stretches of time at computers, we think this could prove to be a powerful match.

Let me show you an example of Richard's writing from that fall. Sarah prompts him to write an original story about anything he wanted. Richard warms to the task and energetically drafts page after page of a story titled "The House." Here is an excerpt, as he wrote it:

Then it was a school Feild trip into the woods to camp out. They had to go on this Feild trip. Then they got all their thigs that they needed For this. So then the day came. it took 1 Full day to get where we need to go. So then once we got there we had a great veiw of a lake and then night came the Five kids went around the huge campFire where everyone told scary stories.

Sarah evaluates the story using a rubric developed by Lipson and Wixson.[32] In her analysis of Richard's work, she notes difficulties with capitalization, punctuation, and structure. She also notes that his use of tense and voice are inconsistent. Moreover, run-on sentences abound, and at the end of the story, the reader is left confused about the plot.

Sarah's analysis of Richard's expository writing sample proves even more revealing. She instructs him to "write about something familiar." When he decides to write about soccer, Sarah urges him to write as if she (the reader) doesn't know anything about the sport. Below is a copy of Richard's composition, as he wrote it:

> You can not use your hands except iF you are throwing in the ball like when you are throwing in the all you bring your hands back behind your head with the ball in your hand, and then you try to throw it very Far or to a teammate.
>
> A red card is not very good you don't want to get a red card to get a red card you swear at the reF or you hit someone like with your Fist or you kick them.

Sarah analyzes the piece according to composing and mechanical skills.[33] The composing rubric takes into account the quality of ideas, organization, diction, sentence and paragraph structure. Richard scores in the low range in all areas except the quality of his ideas. In sum, as Sarah points out, Richard's writing is informative but lacks organization. His piece would also benefit from an introductory paragraph, a more robust structure, and transitional words and phrases. When Sarah asks him to review his work, he does so, but doesn't attempt to make revisions. Some of Richard's patterns in writing expository text are consistent with those discussed in the narrative writing sample (i.e., run-on sentences and poor punctuation).

Websites That Connect Students with Authors

When I was growing up, authors seemed to be other-worldly people who sat behind Royal typewriters pounding out books. Happily, today many children's authors have their own websites; some even respond to children's letters. If you have students, like Richard, who become enamored of a particular author, these resources are for you.

- **J. K. Rowling**, author of the *Harry Potter* series (See *www.Scholastic.com*)
- **Roald Dahl,** author of *Charlie and the Chocolate Factory* and *James and the Giant Peach* (See *www.roalddahl.com*)
- Authors and Illustrators from **Verna Aardema** to **Charlotte Zolotow** (See *www.dalton.org/libraries/fairrosa/cl.authors.html*)
- **Author biographies** at the Los Angeles Public Library, in English and Spanish (See *www.lapl.org/kidsweb/coolsites/ bookauthor-Op.html*)

Possible to Meet a Children's Author?

Many children's book authors are willing to visit schools, which can create an unforgettable experience for students. See if there are any authors in your area who are willing to meet your students and discuss their books. (See *www.snowcrest.net/kidpower/authors2.html*)

Explicit Instruction in Writing in Many Text Genres Analysis of Richard's writing samples reveal a child on the brink of adolescence who needs explicit writing instruction and extensive opportunities to write in multiple genres. Since he enjoys using computers we decide to integrate them, along with telecommunication tools, into his literacy instruction. Our aim is to both engage Richard's interest in improving his writing and to give him a new purpose for writing clear, well-elaborated texts.

Richard also needs to strengthen his reading skills. To that end, he and Sarah soon settle on *Harry Potter and the Sorcerer's Stone.* When Richard reads about the invented sport, Quidditch, he is transfixed. As every Harry Potter fan knows, Quidditch is a sport that Harry and his friends at Hogwarts Academy compete in on a playing field that's far above the treetops. Players zoom around on broomsticks that are powered by magical forces. Harry became a "seeker," a coveted position in which the player chases the lightning-fast "golden snitch."

As a first step toward writing an expository piece about Quidditch, Richard creates a K-W-L chart (see the figure on page 126). Next he learns how to use the software program, Inspiration, to create a graphic organizer to explain to the novice the complexities of the sport.

What I KNOW *about* Quidditch	What I WANT *to know about* Quidditch
Broomsticks	Rules
Many balls	Positions
Hoop/goal	How to win
Goalie	Number on a team
Bat/stick	Equipment
Chaser—ball with wings	Scoring–how and how much
	History

What I LEARNED *about* Quidditch

Quidditch is a game from the book *Harry Potter.* It is a game played high up in the air with the players flying around on brooms. It's like a combination of soccer and basketball and a little of hockey. For more information read the book *Harry Potter* or check out our map on Quidditch.

Richard's K-W-L Chart

Richard is eager to post each of these creations on his personal web page on the Lab website. In contrast to most of the younger students, he grasps the vastness of the Internet. Lots of people "out there" could discover his work and read it! This revolutionary thought motivates Richard to create his own All-Star Quidditch team and post his ideas.

SpicyTaco's All-Star Quidditch Team

CHASERS: Kobe Bryant
Michael Jordan
Magic Johnson
KEEPER: Brian Dofoe
SEEKER: Emmitt Smith
BEATERS: Mia Hamm
Sammy Sosa

With his growing awareness of the power of the web, SpicyTaco adds these sentences:

> Can you beat my All-Star team?
> E-mail me with your best shot!

A boy named Celtic becomes interested in SpicyTaco's Quidditch team. Here is Celtic's first message (as he wrote it):

> well i think my quidditch team can beat yours here goes: chasers:
> Ron Mercer, bob cousy, M.J.
> keeper: patrick Roy
> seeker: terrel Davis
> 2 beaters: Mark Mcguire and larry walker.
> So do you like the celtics? They are my favorite team. Have read all
> of the Harry Potter books? I finished the third yesterday. C-ya

SpicyTaco responds, with only minor coaching and help with the editing process by Sarah.

> *Dear Celtic,*
>
> Your team sounds good but. . . my team sounds a little better. I think
> Terrel Davis is a good seeker because I watch him play for the Bronco's.
> He is almost as good as Emmitt Smith but not quite as tough.
>
> I don't really, like the Boston Celtics. They aren't my favorite
> team. My favorite team is the L.A. Lakers.
>
> I didn't read all the Harry Potter books yet, but I really want to
> read them. I just finished the first one. I like the part when they go
> into the forbidden forest. What was your favorite part? Did you like
> the second book?
> Write back soon. Thanks.
>
> SpicyTaco

Richard's reply suggests that he has learned the conventions of letter writing with continued practice over time. Also, he is highly motivated to come across as both cool and smart. He invites further discussion at the end of his message by relating the scene he liked best in book one of the series and then asking Celtic for his opinion of book two. Consistent with the genre, Richard also uses a salutation and closes with "Write back soon. Thanks," before signing his name.

Over time, Richard's correspondence with Celtic becomes increasingly personal, and references to sports are shifted to the end of the message. In this message Richard begins with sports, offers glimpses into his personal life, and then—most gratifying of all—takes on the voice of a literary critic in referring to his favorite scene from book one. Richard writes the following :

Dear Celtic,

I like the Lakers, but people out here don't really like them. Most of the people out here like the Celtics. I guess from your name you do too. Where do you live anyway? I live outside Boston in the suburbs.

How was your Christmas? Did you get your shopping done? Well I had an ok Christmas. My parents had a lot of parties. What did you do on New Year's Eve? I just stayed home with my brother and watched it on TV. I thought it was ok.

I haven't read the second and third Harry Potter books yet. Should I read them? Are they any good? My favorite part in Harry Potter and the Sorcerer's Stone was when the kids got a detention and had to go into the forest as their punishment. It had the best action in the book.

As for Quidditch, the position I would chose to be is a Beater because they get to beat things with their sticks.

Your friend,
SpicyTaco

In writing "best action of the book" Richard takes Celtic's perspective into account; he assumes that Celtic has read the entire book.

If we fast-forward to the boys' final exchange, we can detect a more mature style in Richard's letter-style email message. Note that he doesn't begin with a salutation this time, which may reflect an increased sense of familiarity. Harry Potter only rates a brief mention; the boys now concentrate on "kid culture." Here's what Richard writes:

I haven't read the second and third one yet but I hope to read them sometime soon. What grade are you in and how old are you? I am just wondering. I am 13 and I am in 7th grade. I haven't ever been to Denver and I like the broncos too but my favorite team is the Dallas Cowboys. Who is your favorite player on the Denver Broncos? I always come to Harvard because I have this literacy lab. It's fun and I love Harvard. Going around there with my family is cool.

A friend,
SpicyTaco

Richard's progress as a writer is quite rapid. While having opportunities to write to a large audience motivates him, the explicit, one-on-one instruction Sarah provides is also essential to his success. The research project may provide a new context for applying skills, but developing the skills is a priority in every session at the Lab.

Online Peer Review

Would you like your students to participate in peer review with other students around the country? If so, these university-based resources may help you get started:

1. A **ThinkQuest** called Collab-o-Write invites students to add to a story or illustrate a story with their original compositions. Middle school students may appreciate the fact that the site was created by students like themselves. (See *www.thinkquest.org/library/lib/site_sum_outside.html?tname=2626 &url=2626/*)

2. **Calibrated Peer Review**, developed at the University of California, Los Angeles, invites students to first critique three nonfiction reports written by others across the country; then students can submit their own paper for review. (See *moisci.ucla.edu*)

3. Check out easy avenues, such as school intranets and bulletin boards, which are available through companies such as **Blackboard** and **WebCT**. Students can post their drafts and read their classmates' work. (Sites are password protected.)[34]

When I [Nicole] take over Richard's instruction in the spring, I make every effort to continue to build on Richard's emerging sense of audience. In particular, I focus on the novel *Jip*, a book by Katherine Paterson that won a Scott O'Dell Award. Given that *Jip* is a work of historical fiction, it's conducive to literature studies both in narrative and expository genres. For example, the setting of the book is the Civil War era in rural Vermont. The novel touches on topics as broad-based as early schooling, slavery, and the laws of the time. (Coincidentally, Richard is studying slavery and the Civil War in school.) On the expository side, I encourage Richard to respond to the book by adapting the story in some way. He decides to set the novel in contemporary times, and composes an original story titled "A Multi-Millionaire Jip in the Year 2000."

Anticipating a national audience for his work, Richard works hard. He composes his story at the computer. Then he creates his own writing rubric (with my help) as a guide for editing the mechanics of the piece (i.e., capitalization, spelling).

A Multi-Millionaire Jip in the Year 2000

"And are you satisfied that it remains so? Even when there might even be a chance however infinitesimal that you are meant for something else far better than this?" Jip has a new chance for a completely new life in New York in the year 2000. Now here are some ideas about Jip living in New York in the year 2000.

Jip is the new Multi-Millionaire in New York! When Jip was at the farm he had no money whatsoever, but now he is the new Multi-Millionaire in New York. At the farm he had to ride in a wooden wagon. In the year 2000, Jip now rides in some new hot wheels like a BMW. On the farm he worked hard, but now in the year 2000 he sits back and watches TV at home. On the farm Jip wore dirty farmer clothes, but in the year 2000 he has some silk threads, while walking down the street.

Some people he hangs out with are cool. Jip had one best friend named Sheldon, now in New York he has a ton of cool friends. On the farm Jip worked with animals very well. Now in the year 2000 he works with co-workers and computers. On the farm Jip was very weak but very friendly. Now in the year 2000 he works out every day and is still very nice.

Now these are some of the contrasts of Jip in Vermont and Jip in the year 2000 in New York. If you wish, you may add in any other ideas you have about this book.

This story was inspired by Jip, His Story, by Katherine Paterson. See the brainstorming Web and formal Outline I used to write this story!

Richard's "Jip" story is posted on his web page. He is thrilled when he sees it, and begins to anticipate the email messages he might receive from readers.

Did the Jip project, and its eventual inclusion on his web page, stimulate Richard's interest in reading? Apparently so. His mother remarks, "He mentioned that he was very excited about his project. He enjoys so much this book [Jip]. I was so excited. You introduced him to reading. He talks about it. He opens the book and reads all the way to school."[35]

But Richard not only reads more; he writes more, too, partly because other people will be reading and perhaps even responding to his work. Thus, over the school year he learns how to anticipate the needs of his readership and respond to the email messages they inspired.

From this point forward, I [Nicole] don't think Richard will be content to write for only a single reader. He's had a taste of the excitement inherent in exchanging ideas with others by publishing his work for a larger audience that he envisioned in his mind's eye. I hope he will submit his work to web-based publishing venues, such as e-'zines and book review sites for adolescents, in the future.

MORE EYE-OPENERS

These literacy adventures on the Internet have taught me [Julie Wood] several other lessons, which I [Julie] hope will be helpful for *your* forays into cyberspace.

Many Lab students appropriated telecommunication tools for their own purposes. In particular, they envisioned their personal web pages as a way to:

- Share their expertise with others (e.g., the best Pokemon websites)
- Display a sense of humor (as in describing a funny incident)
- Display passion for a subject (e.g., wrestling, a favorite pet)
- Develop a unique voice as a writer

In general, Lab students used email capabilities:

- As a promotional tool for their writing
- To correspond with a peer about a favorite book, and learn more about him or her in the process
- To publish a book review

- To establish a dialog with their lab teachers by sending them messages from home
- To write to family members from the Lab

Here are several other compelling reasons why you might want to use telecommunication tools to support literacy development, even though the investment of time and money is admittedly steep. Students made great strides. In general, they:

- Created more elaborate texts when writing for their web page, or composing an email message, than when writing for more traditional purposes
- Were motivated to publish their work on the Web
- Appreciated the professional look their writing took on when they used word processing and illustration tools
- Showed greater interest in corresponding, via email with friends and acquaintances than with people they didn't know
- Used original artwork as a jumping off point for communicating with others

A FINAL NOTE

As you can see from these vignettes, *teachers are the real avatars of change;* it's teachers who are the most influential when it comes to transforming literacy instruction by figuring out smart ways to use digital technologies—ways that have profound implications for learning.

To make the best choices, teachers need many opportunities to learn from each other. They also need plenty of time. According to the findings from a ten-year Apple Classroom of Tomorrow (ACOT) study,

> Teachers need increased and varied opportunities to see other teachers, to confront their actions and examine their motives, and to reflect critically on the consequences of their choices, decisions and actions. They need opportunities for ongoing dialogue about their experiences and for continuous development of their abilities to imagine and discover more powerful learning experiences for their students.[36]

The teachers (graduate students) in the Lab study documented in this section did in fact have opportunities to cross-pollinate their ideas.

Yet, most remarked that it wasn't always easy to change their practice in tune with the twenty-first century. The Lab teachers taught me many things that may resonate with your own professional development experiences. In general, Lab teachers:

- Became more thoughtful about the give and take of adding new tools to support literacy instruction
- Began to strategize with parents about how to use computers at home (when available) to extend the reading and writing experiences in the Lab
- Thought more expansively about how to embed computers and telecommunication tools into their teaching in ways that made sense
- Invented ways to adapt technology to meet the needs of their students (e.g., creating an interactive dialog journal, receiving direct feedback from their students about the Lab experience, and helping students develop a sense of audience)

As those of you involved in professional development know, making these sorts of pedagogical leaps speaks to the dedication of the Lab teachers and their willingness to update their practice for the digital age. Here are a few questions for you to consider in light of your teaching situation. *How can I support teachers as they gain mastery as innovators by inventing their own creative strategies? How can I create environments that offer teachers many opportunities to spread the word?*

I hope that by joining forces we can keep these questions at the forefront of a national debate on how best to educate all students for the world they will inhabit in 2020.

ENDNOTES

1. *Michelin New England* (Greenville, SC: Michelin Travel Publications, 1997), 149–151.
2. M. Keller, "Bigger Than Ever," *Boston Globe*, 2001, October 21, E1–2.
3. *ibid.*, E1
4. *ibid.*, E1
5. *ibid.*
6. Victoria Purcell-Gates, "Process Teaching with Direct Instruction and Feedback in a University-Based Clinic." In Ellen McIntyre and

Michael Pressley (eds.), *Balanced Instruction: Strategies and Skills in Whole Language*. (Norwood, MA: Christopher-Gordon, 1996), 109.

7. Frank Smith, *Joining the Literacy Club: Further Essays into Education* (Portsmouth, NH: Heinemann, 1987).

8. All children in the Lab selected their own pseudonyms (e.g., Cecily Salamander) for publishing work on the Web and corresponding via email.

9. K-W-L is a technique designed to improve students' comprehension by having them organize their ideas into three columns: what they Know, what they Want to know, and what they Learned about a topic of interest (Ogle, 1989).

10. Linda Rath, Personal Communication, November 2001.

11. Victoria Purcell-Gates, Personal Communication, 1997. In the 1995–96 academic year, for example, students attending the Lab scored on average in the 25.9th percentile in the fall, and the 46.7th percentile in the spring. In just 7 months and fewer than 40 hours of Lab instruction, the group went from being well below average readers (as measured by a norm-referenced test) to demonstrating solidly average reading achievement.

12. As of this writing, the Harry Potter series has made publishing history with the sales from the fifth book in the series, *Harry Potter and the Order of the Phoenix*. *TIME* notes the phenomenal appeal of Harry Potter books to children, including students who struggle with reading. Reporter Nancy Gibbs remarks, "Children buy J. K. Rowling's books with their own money. They wear out flashlights reading them after lights-out. Kids with a fear of fat books and dyslexia kids who have never finished a book read Harry Potter not once or twice but dozens of times." ("The Real Magic of Harry Potter," TIME June 23, 2003), 63.

13. Quoted by Alvin Powell (May 26, 1998), "Race, Culture, Important Issues for Conference" (Cambridge, MA: *Harvard.net.news*, a publication of the Harvard Conference on the Internet and Society), 6.

14. Abbreviations and quotation from "Rest Assured—Students, Teachers, and Language Are 'Alive and Kickin'," *The Council Chronicle*, National Council of Teachers of English, Vol. 12, No. 4, May, 2003, 5.

15. For security reasons children's exact identities were never revealed. When helping students edit their email messages and autobiographies, we asked them to delete their street addresses, phone numbers,

and so on. Likewise we avoided using photographs and had students create self-portraits either with online art tools (such as KidPix) or by drawing with colored markers. The latter images were scanned into each web page by our web masters.

16. Another important point about security: All messages sent to children via email, all book reviews, and all messages entered into the guest book were carefully screened by teachers, the web masters, and myself.

17. I was interested to read an article in the "Circuits" section of the *New York Times* that described the experience of 50 fifth-graders and their teachers in Taylorsville, North Carolina. The teachers and students had posted an email message asking for people around the world to write to their children as part of a geography project. The children received an astonishing number of messages—half a million! —that included people at NASA, the Pentagon, and a Peace Corps volunteer in Turkistan. (Heidi A. Schuessler, "Social Studies Class Finds How Far E-Mail Travels," *New York Times*, February 22, 2001, Circuits section, 8.)

18. For an excellent account of the history of email, developed in part right here in Cambridge, MA (at BBN Corporation) see the *New York Times* article by Katie Hafner titled "Billions Served Daily, and Counting" (December 6, 2001) at the online archive.

19. Interview, March 28, 2000.

20. Kristin Kellogg Valdmanis and Nicole Jernée, former Lab teachers and research assistants, contributed to this chapter by writing case studies of two of our students.

21. Sherry Turkle, *The Second Self* (New York: Simon and Schuster 1984).

22. Peter Elbow, *Writing with Power* (New York: Oxford University Press, 1981).

23. Donald H. Graves, *A Fresh Look at Writing* (Portsmouth, NH: Heinemann, 1994), 81.

24. Ralph Fletcher, *What a Writer Needs* (Portsmouth, NH: Heinemann, 1993), 68.

25. I have also written about Medo's case for a publication by Educational Development Center called "Computers and Process Writing: A Marriage Waiting to Happen." The entire text can be found at *www.edtechleaders.org/Resources/Readings/UpperElem.Literacy/ Wood_computersWriting.htm*

26. Case report, Emily, 2000, 1–2.

27. Marjorie Y. Lipson and Karen K. Wixson, *Assessment & Instruction of Reading and Writing Disability*, 2nd ed. (Reading, MA: Addison Wesley Longman, 1997).

28. Emily's case report, 13.

29. Fall case report, 15.

30. *Ibid.*, 18.

31. In some cases I have used Nicole Jernée's exact wording. Nicole drew upon the case report written by Sarah Darnton, Richard's former Lab teacher.

32. *Op. cit.*, 366–67.

33. Again, Sarah used a rubric developed by Lipson and Wixson, 1997.

34. Guernsey, L. (August 14, 2003), A Young Writers' Roundtable, via the Web. *New York Times*, E1 and E6.

35. Parent interview, May 17, 2000.

36. *Op. cit.*, Sandholtz, Ringstaff, and Dwyer, 1997, 51.

4

Becoming an (Even More) Innovative Literacy Professional

Knowledge must come through action; you can have no test which is not fanciful, save by trial.

—Sophocles

REFLECTING ON YOUR PAST, PRESENT, AND FUTURE

One of my favorite paintings in Boston's Museum of Fine Arts was painted by Paul Gauguin, in Tahiti, over a century ago. Entitled, *Where Do We Come From? What Are We? Where Are We Going?* it's a sprawling canvas depicting three ages of man.[1] What's particularly striking about the painting is that Gauguin addresses us directly, and poses these three questions in French—*D'où venons-nous? Que sommes-nous? D'où allons-nous?* The painting, which Gauguin considered his masterpiece, has a dreamlike quality, inviting deep contemplation about the meaning of life. It may seem a stretch to invoke these questions when thinking about the practical aspects of integrating technology into your reading and language arts curricula, and yet we do need to examine the past, present, and future to create an effective plan. What has worked well for you in the past? Where are you right now? What is your vision for the future?

Once you've figured out answers to these questions, you'll be well on your way to becoming a change agent in your school or district. This section of the book is designed to help you *begin* the process, which is sometimes the most challenging task of all. Once you build momentum, you'll be able to devise your own brainstorming worksheets and plans for not just one school year, but perhaps for three school years. Taking the long view can pay off handsomely. For example, if in year 1, you applied for a fourth-grade laptop computer program, in year 2 you could implement a writers' workshop in your classroom. By adding a wireless connection in year 3 (to allow for Internet access), you could expand your writing program into the content area themes.

The good news is that this is an amazing time to be rethinking your literacy teaching. A wealth of free, well-thought-out professional development tools await you, via the Internet. Some of the resources you'll need to craft a plan are listed in this chapter; others, such as creating your own classroom website, appear in text boxes sprinkled throughout the book.

GETTING STARTED

Given the choice between changing and proving there's no need to do so,
almost everybody will get busy on the proof.
—John Kenneth Galbraith

Begin by conducting your own research project to find out who the movers and shakers are in your immediate area. Who is creating a buzz around literacy and educational technology in your school district? Seek out this expert and observe him or her in action. Take notes. Schedule time to meet with local technology coordinators and literacy specialists. Let them know you're interested in expanding your teaching repertoire and would appreciate their help and advice.

FIND A BUDDY, IN YOUR DISTRICT OR IN CYBERSPACE

Extend your reading and writing program beyond the boundaries of your school district. You may teach in Seattle but your kindred spirit, educationally speaking, may be in Kalamazoo. How will you ever find him or her? Try to go to a conference on educational technologies. Invest energy in a distance learning course on integrating literacy for the digital age, some of which offer graduate credit.

Opportunities to Connect with Other Educators

- The **Chatboard Network** for posting messages and receiving feedback: Post on "Hot Topics." (See *www.teachers.net/chatboard*)
- **Teacher to Teacher** offers moderated professional chats focused on children's literature, teaching with technology and more. (See *teachers.scholastic.teacher*)
- The **Knowledge Loom** is a comprehensive site with information about best practices and opportunities for online discussions. (See *knowledgeloom.org*)
- The **International Reading Association** (IRA) invites teachers to discuss how they integrate new technologies into their reading and language arts curricula, with a particular focus on struggling readers and writers. Anyone with an email account can subscribe to this discussion group, called RTEACHER. (To join, see *www.reading.org/publications/journals/RT/rteacherdirections.html*)

STAY ON TOP OF NEW DEVELOPMENTS IN LITERACY AND TECHNOLOGY

Be sure to subscribe to publications that review the types of software products and websites that are closely aligned with your reading and writing programs. Two of my favorite magazines are *Children's Software & New Media Revue* and *Classroom Connect*. Also, become an innovation-watcher by following the business section and/or technology column in your local newspaper (e.g., the "Circuits" section of the *New York Times* that appears on Thursdays, which is also available online).

Two Excellent Publications That Can Save You Hours of Planning

- *Children's Software & New Media Revue*. (See *www.childrenssoftware.com*)
- *Classroom Connect: The K-12 Educators' Guide to the Internet*. (See *www.classroom.com*)

"MAKE A NEW PLAN, STAN... "

... as singer/songwriter Paul Simon wrote. Thirty-six weeks. That's what the school year consists of, typically, in public schools. Each month has its own character, from a *tabula rasa* feeling in September to a race-to-the-finish mood in June. How can you use the unique character of each of your thirty-six weeks best to promote literacy learning in your classroom?

Design a Plan That Includes "Cross Threads"

Begin by identifying several long-term initiatives that you'd like to launch in the fall that you can build on throughout the school year. I call these long-term projects *cross threads*. One cross thread might involve collecting students' writing samples and saving them in an online portfolio. If you begin this project early, you'll have an entire year's worth of data to use as part of your assessment program. Or, you might decide that you want to build (or revamp) a classroom website for publishing student work. If you do, your website will pay dividends all year long.

What Type of Plan?

Next, decide whether you want to take a slow approach to adding media to your literacy program by adapting the "Ease Into It Plan," or a more ambitious "Turbo Plan." It all depends on where you are now, how much time you feel you can commit to developing new programs, and how many resources you have available to you.

Projects for the Ease Into It Plan could include two cross threads and then two or three special projects that you launch during the school year. The special projects should map onto your overarching literacy goals for the year. For example, if improved writing is your focus, students could:

- Create photo journals in the fall
- Write nonfiction articles during the winter, via a WebQuest
- Develop their "voice" as writers by corresponding with e-pals in another country in the spring

You might decide to showcase student learning by hosting an Open House for Families and Friends in the spring. You can use the Brainstorming activity sheet (in this section) to help you devise a plan.

Resources for Literacy Initiatives

- Check out these **WebQuests** specifically geared for promoting literacy. (See *www.oswego.org/staff/cchamber/literacy/webquest.cfm*)
- For cross-cultural writing exchanges, find a match at **ePals**. (See *www.epals.com*)
- **Shared Writing** on the Internet (as described in a text box in Part 3, "Richard's Story").
- Join **book discussions** with classrooms from all over the globe through Book Rap. (See *rite.ed.au/oz-teachernet/projects/book-rap*)
- **Outta Ray's Head**, created by Canadian teacher/librarian Ray Saitz, will help you use new technologies to breathe new life into writing, literature, and poetry instruction. (See *www.rayser.ca/*)
- Mrs. Silverman, an innovative second-grade teacher has amassed **Internet projects from all over the world** into one "Webfolio." Use these to help you create your own vision. (See *kids-learn.org*)
- **Poetry, children's literature, and tips for helping parents read with their students.** These and other goodies have been assembled by the Oswego City School District in New York. Be sure to see the links to Internet Projects and Literature Guides. (See *oswego.org/staff/cchamber/literacy/index.cfm*)

If you're ready for the Turbo Plan, you could plan to initiate a different project every other month focused on the same goal (e.g., improved writing instruction). Instead of planning *two* cross threads and *three* major initiatives for the school year, you might decide to have *three* cross threads (by adding a classroom newspaper to the fall initiatives, for example) and launching a new project *every two months*.

Additional writing and technology projects might include:

- Using word processors to support process writing
- Engaging students in peer review of their writing using the Internet
- Exploring the vocabulary websites discussed previously and devising creative ways to use new words in written compositions (which students then post on the classroom website)

SHOWCASING STUDENT LEARNING

You might decide to orchestrate two events to showcase student learning: one in the mid-fall and the other in the spring. In addition to hosting an Open House for Families and Friends, you might also plan an Authors' Night during which students read aloud from their own published books and respond to questions about how their ideas developed. You can use the Brainstorming activity sheet (in this section) to devise a plan.

FUNDING YOUR VISION

Money. Yes, well, this can be a problem. Do you dream of having a laptop program to help students develop their writing skills? Would your students benefit from literary projects involving digital camcorders and/or digital cameras, but your district's budget cuts make such ideas seem impossible? Keep in mind the fact that many businesses and foundations are interested in underwriting the cost of integrating educational technologies into schools. How-to books and other online resources can show you how to go about securing funds to realize your vision. When you think about it, knowing how to go after funding sources is a professional skill that will serve you well throughout your teaching career. Fortunately, once you prove yourself with your first grant, you'll have a better shot at receiving subsequent funding.

Polishing Your Grant Writing Skills

- See the **International Society for Technology in Education's** (ISTE) Resources and Tips for Grant Writers. (See *www.iste.org/resources/funding/index.cfm*)
- Designed specifically for educators, a site called **School Grants** offers resources and tips for K–12 teachers to apply for grants.(See *www.schoolgrants.org*)
- See the **Philanthropy News Digest-K-12 Funding Opportunities** to stay up-to-date on funding opportunities. (See *fdncenter.org/funders/*)

In addition, these two books can help you achieve your goals from start to finish.

- Jim Burke and Carol Ann Prater, **I'll Grant You That** (Portsmouth, NH: Heinemann, 2000).
- Cynthia Knowles, **The First-Time Grantwriter's Guide to Success** (Thousand Oaks, CA: Corwin, 2002).

BE PATIENT

It takes time to become an innovative teacher of reading and writing. And some of your colleagues may be naysayers. You will need to develop skin as thick as rhinoceros hide, to paraphrase Eleanor Roosevelt. Be bold; have the courage of your convictions. Share your new teaching literacy techniques with your most skeptical colleagues and invite them to collaborate. Be generous with your resources and encourage others to adapt your projects for their students.

BE BRAVE

You will be meeting your students in the twenty-first century, which is where, as educators, our thinking needs to be. Your students' futures depend on their ability to bend and mold new tools in ways that make them better, more confident readers and writers, and more in touch with the world. As their teacher you have a unique opportunity to learn alongside them, making at least as many discoveries, which may profoundly transform your literacy practice. And remember, as Henry Adams remarked nearly a century ago, "A teacher affects eternity; he can never tell where his influence stops."

LET'S CONTINUE THE CONVERSATION

I'm always interested in hearing about the experiences of other literacy professionals when it comes to integrating digital media. If you want to share ideas, please drop me an email message at *Julie.Wood@post. harvard.edu.*

Now go out there and innovate! Get those kids of yours reading and writing like pros, using digital tools as full-fledged members of the digital age.

BRAINSTORMING: CHANGING YOUR TEACHING FOREVER

Here are two worksheets for you and your colleagues to begin or extend the brainstorming phase of your literacy and technology plan. Part A can help you clarify your vision. Part B can help you outline a plan.

Part A: *Fine-tune Your Vision*

1. What do you have going for you right now (i.e., people and resources)?

   A. *Personnel: Advocates and Angels* (e.g., technology coordinators, reading specialists, high-tech parent volunteers)

   B. *Computers and other tools at your disposal* (e.g., digital cameras, digital camcorders, software)

   C. *School structures that are already in place* (e.g., professional development events)

2. Wish list: What do you *really* need to achieve your technology and literacy goals?

   Time (e.g., professional development workshops, time to collaborate, time to plan lessons?)

   Equipment? (e.g., Zip™ drives, digital cameras, projection devices, software)

   Technology support personnel? (Is there someone assigned to help you with day-to-day maintenance and glitches?)

Part B: *Make It Happen*

1. Who can you enlist to help you develop a plan for integrating new technologies into literacy instruction? (e.g., parents, high school students, media specialists)

2. What funding opportunities will you seek?
   A. Local businesses (e.g., banks, high-tech companies)
   B. Grant writing opportunities (local and government)

3. What is your overall plan? *(In the spirit of "getting digital," you and your colleagues might enjoy using electronic resources to capture brainstorming sessions and record your plan. If so, see PBS's TeacherLine, at teacherline.pbs.org, and take advantage of the feature called "My Portfolio.")*

4. What support systems can you design to help you stick to your plan?(e.g., *formal monthly meetings with impromptu sessions in between; setting up listserv just for you and your colleagues and using it to share aha! moments and requests for help*)

5. What additional training would help you achieve your goals? (e.g., *in-service workshops or online courses about process writing, creating online portfolio, editing digital video*)

6. And now for the fun part: How will you show off your students' learning and *your own* learning? (e.g., *classroom website, Technology Open Houses, Technology Fairs, articles in professional journals*)

[1] *Where Do We Come From? What Are We? Where Are We Going?* by Paul Gauguin: Boston's Museum of Fine Art (See *www.mfa.org* and search for this painting).

© 2004 by Julie Wood from *Literacy Online*, Portsmouth, NH: Heinemann.

Sample Brainstorm: The Ease Into It Plan, School Year 20___

SEPTEMBER	OCTOBER	NOVEMBER	DECEMBER	JANUARY	FEBRUARY	MARCH	APRIL	MAY	JUNE
Cross Thread Plan 1 Online writing portfolio	*Cross Thread Plan 2* Revamp classroom website								Culmination of all the cross thread projects
	Special Project 1 Students create photo journals	→—————	→——	*Special Project 2* Students write across the curriculum using a webQuest as a guide		→——	*Special Project 3* Students develop their "voice" by writing to e-pals via email	→—————	
								Showcase Event Technology Open House for families and friends	

© 2004 by Julie Wood from *Literacy Online*, Portsmouth, NH: Heinemann.

Sample Brainstorm: The Turbo Plan, School Year 20____

September	October	November	December	January	February	March	April	May	June
Cross Thread Plan 1 Online writing portfolio	*Cross Thread Plan 2* Revamp classroom website	*Cross Thread Plan 3* Classroom newspaper	→					↑	Culmination of all the cross thread projects
	Special Project 1 Students create photo journals	→	*Special Project 2* Students learn to use word processors for writers' workshop	→	*Special Project 3* Students write across the curriculum using a WebQuest as a guide.	→	*Special Project 4* Students engage in peer review via the Internet		↑ *Special Project 5* Students explore vocabulary websites and use new words in writing
		Showcase Event 1 Technology Open House for family and friends				*Showcase Event 2* authors' night with students' original books			